"Sparklingly intelligent, pliantly sensitive… that's my impression of Sagarpriya.

"I will never forget my experience with her, when she drew out the male and female within me, the two counterpoised parts of myself. It was like magic. The moment she did it, I was amazed and felt as if I had already known this.

"This book can easily take you to a place where you thought you'd never reach, even though you had a vague idea of where it might be."

Banana Yoshimoto

The two shores of Love

inner man & inner woman

Sagarpriya DeLong

With assistance from Nitya Cristiana Allievi

Drawings by Sidd Murray-Clark

Ecstatic Silence
PUBLICATIONS

Cover Design: Shivananda Ackermann
Cover Photo: Devayan Henriksen
Editor: Sarito Carol Neiman
Designer and Compositor: Francesca Komel
Ebook Development: Antonio Savorelli

ISBN: 979-12-200-0466-4

To

the Presence—
nameless, faceless,
never born and never dying

Contents

The two shores of Love

inner man & inner woman

Sagarpriya DeLong

Author's Preface

It is unbelievable how many methods there are on the market today that help you to "know yourself." It has become almost impossible to choose among them. And each one suggests something you have to do or practice in order to achieve the goal. Naturally, if you are interested in knowing yourself, you try this and that. Or, to express it more personally, I was once the consumer and I tried. Certainly I became more knowledgeable about myself, and I experienced resolutions to certain hang-ups. But the central thing eluded me and, like others, I became a little fed up with the search, ready to choose "none of the above" and settle down into the life I was already leading as best I could.

By chance I met Osho. I wasn't looking for a spiritual master, but by good fortune I found him—or perhaps he found me. He taught me that if I wanted to know myself, the key was to "rest" in myself, not to "do." And over quite a few years of being his sannyasin, I discovered by this resting process that there isn't really the kind of self I expected to find, something like a substance or a thing, but rather two polar opposite energies, the male and female, which have the potential to dance with each other, to enjoy each other's company, and in this way to create an atmosphere of love that is unimaginably beautiful.

In this book I am proposing a way for you to find your own experience of this love. Although I am the creator of the method you will be reading about, Star Sapphire Energywork, I am also its first client. This is why I write the book in first person. My experimentation was so intimate that I cannot describe it to you in any other way. I am sharing my own process, through a number of personal anecdotes and recollections. Even when I am giving a session to someone else, I myself am growing with that person. This is why, when you read one of the samples featured in a box, it is written in the present tense—to give this flavor of being there, being part of it, being involved.

Once you become aware that you have two counterpoised aspects, male and female, you will discover in the same moment that there is a rift between them. In almost everyone, they are at war. It is not necessarily a hot war. In myself, one was dominant (the female) and the other was collapsed (the male). The male had actually gone to sleep, finding this the most convenient choice given the situation, and the female had become grey with the tiredness of doing everything alone. If you look closely, this is a political game—and which one do you think is the winner? Fritz Perls used to say, "The underdog always wins." But winning is not worth much.

Actually, the real politics is within you. We can see very well the politics that is outside. We see the countries vying with each other, scrambling to be the victors on many fronts, economical, political, social. And we see the wars that arise when an attempted domination is not received with enthusiasm. These wars are simply a reflection of what is going on deep inside each individual. When individuals change—that is, you and me—and each person becomes a fountain of love inside, wars will simply be impossible.

Star Sapphire Energywork is an outgrowth of my study of the body by means of psychic massage, and my psychological study of myself and others using Osho's idea of resting into truth. I will be explaining in this book how you too can perceive the messages coming from other people's bodies, and I will be sharing with you many of the insights that arose in me because I was Osho's disciple. But you do not need to have a spiritual master yourself to gain benefit from what is proposed. The method is universally applicable.

Besides myself and Osho (in absentia, because he left his body in 1990), there is a third collaborator in this book. Nitya Cristiana Allievi aided me with her considerable talents as a journalist in preparing the Italian version. Nitya was familiar with Star Sapphire as a client, and she was eager that this material should reach a larger audience. She engaged herself with the task of adapting my words in such a way that the Italian reader could be entertained. Her influence can be felt in the English version as well, because she convinced me to eliminate passages that were too technical. Some things I intended for serious students of this work had to be sacrificed, so that an inexperienced person would be swept along from one chapter to the next without any difficulty.

Nitya's contribution to what you are about to read is the lightness, mine is the gravity, and Osho's is… the breeze.

Sagarpriya
Milan, Italy

CHAPTER 1

Introduction to the Inner Male and Female

L ove is a topic that catches everybody's interest. Just look around—it's in the films, in the music, in the magazines. Often before you realize it, you find your eyes fixed on a billboard advertising the latest love story. Or even if it's not your habit, you sometimes glance at the stories of celebrities who have "found each other." In short, everybody is caught by the power of love because it is one of the most exciting things that can happen to a person. The attraction between the two sexes is so magnetic, the absorption is so total, that you want to completely lose yourself in it. That's why, if you have someone to love, who loves you too, you do everything you can to keep that person in your life. Or, if you don't have a partner, the thing you want most in the world is to find one!

But the more experiences you have in relationships, the more you notice that you always confront exactly the same sort of problems—and you don't know what to do about it. When things don't go well with your partner, you can feel almost suffocated. Or sometimes you feel that you have only duties, expectations to fulfill. Or you have to chase after the other one... Whatever type of dynamic repeats itself, the sensation that accompanies it is heaviness and lack of freedom. In moments like that, when everything seems so hopeless, you would like to escape—anything else than to have a relationship!

Usually, you think that the cause of difficulty is that you have found the wrong partner, you have made a mistake in the choice. And you continue to think that sooner or later, you will find the "right" mate for yourself and then everything will work!

Maybe. But actually, the hope for a perfect partner is superficial; the roots of relationship are much deeper, buried in the unconscious part of you. For sure success in relationship, it is best to look there.

Two polarities reside within you

According to the psychologist Carl Gustav Jung, every woman has inside her unconscious mind an "animus," which is an imprint or "archetype" of a male figure. This male figure doesn't remain forever the same, but he has characteristics that mature as the woman grows psychologically. Similarly, every man has an "anima" with changing—or changeable—female characteristics. These figures of the opposite sex are not necessarily evident in daily life, but they are clearly visible in dreams. Supported by his study of alchemical science, Jung also espoused the idea that everyone has "the sun and the moon" inside; that is, everyone has a male and a female aspect.

Something similar, but not exactly the same, has been my experience too. I came to my conclusions by a very different route than Jung. For many years I gave a type of massage where I was clairvoyantly "seeing" images arising from the energy in the bodies I worked on. Over time, I realized that the impressions were of two types, qualitatively different. For now it is sufficient to say that the images had feminine or masculine characteristics, depending on where I was working on the body. And these were images full of exact detail—including facial expressions, body build, type of dress, and past professional experience.

At the time I discovered the "portraits" of these two contrasting figures, I didn't know much about Jung's ideas. However, I was familiar with the philosophies of the East, including Taoist and Tantric principles, so it was not surprising that an energy of the opposite sex would be hiding in the recesses of the body. What was amazing to me was that *both* the male and female characters were so specifically and graphically represented.

I decided it was important to make my clients aware of them. In the beginning, I was limited to just telling the images that I had seen. For example, one image was of a strong woman in a housedress with a stern face and a big body, shaking her finger at someone—she looked like an unpleasant sort of mother. The opposite figure was a young man, maybe twenty, with a thin and very agile body, going to the market on an errand but enjoying distractions along the way. I could easily imagine the relationship between these two: the woman was dominant and the man, unluckily, had a habit of following her directives. But at that time, I hadn't the tools for bringing these figures to life on a stage or for having them interact together. It was only later that I found methods by which the client could experience for himself his masculine and feminine parts, and this was already much better than just hearing about their existence from me.

How they determine your choice of an outer partner in life

Along the way, I learned that the relationship which you see on the inside, between the two polarities, is the same as exists on the outside. For example, in myself I discovered that the male part inside me would have liked to stop school at an early age. In fact, because I was not at all listening to my male part at that time, I continued on a very intellectual path, following a course in philosophy at a select American university, for years pouring my energy into being a good student. But later, when I got married, I chose a man who had dropped out of school at the age of 16. And when I married for the second time it was the same, and also in the third relationship. All the men were very intelligent, but they had all quit their formal education at age 16!

After I became acquainted with my inner man, I discovered that he is attracted to the materials from which you build houses—wood, stone, plaster, tile—and if he could choose his ideal work, it would be carpentry. Also, he likes to find practical solutions to mechanical problems. On the surface of myself, I have always believed that I cannot even change a light bulb. And yet, all of the men in my life have been carpenters or handymen, and some, at other moments in their life, have also been mechanics!

It doesn't happen only to me. So often I will hear a client say, "My inner woman is just like my wife," or sometimes, "That's exactly the way my girlfriend would express herself." This is not an accident; there is an urge within us to unite our masculine and feminine energies, to make them one. And so a man will search outside for the person most appropriate for him, which means similar to his inner woman. A woman will find a man with the characteristics of her inner male. In a whole crowd of people, you are able to eliminate hundreds until your choice finally narrows down to one and you know for sure that's *it*!

This is particularly true when you get married. When you decide to commit yourself to someone in a deeper or longer way, it is always because you see your "opposite side" in them. Perhaps you are not conscious of it; perhaps you are even critical of this person, but there is the feeling that you cannot go away from them even if you would like to. This correspondence doesn't always apply with boyfriends or girlfriends. But actually, in many more cases than you might think, your partner even when you are not married is providing you with a mirror of your hidden side.

Contacting your male and female through a series of ten questions

It is possible, if you like, to experience your own masculine and feminine sides now, using a simple method. You will be answering questions, and it works better if you have a friend with you to listen. The listener should be someone who is not emotionally involved with you—the reasons will be clear when the questions are presented.

It might seem strange, but you will speak from each eye, one at a time. The eyes are like windows, giving access to the two energies, even if the roots of the two energies are deeper in the body. The right eye connects to the masculine energy, the left to the feminine.

Now you can cover the right eye with one hand, or if you wear glasses, just put a handkerchief inside as a cover. We are going to start with the left eye which remains open; this is the feminine side. Ready?

The questions:

1. How do you feel now that someone is looking at you and listening to you?

2. How do you see the room in which you find yourself? Do you like the colors, do you find it warm or cold?

3. Which kinds of activity make you happy?

4. Do you like the place where you live? Speak about all the aspects—the type of house or apartment, the light inside, the garden (or lack of), the neighbors, the country, the continent… Would you like to change location?

5. Do you work? (The question has to be asked this way, because sometimes only one side of the body is working.) If you have a work, which aspects of it are you doing? Do you like this work, or would you like to change job?

6. What are the priorities in your life?—first, second, and third, and whatever comes after.

7. Do you have enough space in daily life to develop your interests and express your creativity?

8. If you have a relationship, how is it for you? Did you choose your partner in the beginning? Are you in love with your partner now?

9. Are there things you have to do which you don't like? And if you didn't have to do them, what would you do with the spare time?

10. Is there anything else you would like to say, now that you have a listener?

Take a short break. Then cover the left eye so that you can speak from the right eye—the masculine side—and let your friend read the questions again.

You will notice that your answers are completely different. It's good to have two energies that choose different things! There are twenty-four hours in a day, and you can manage to let both have the space to express themselves. Once when I did this exercise with a friend of mine, he understood that his male side would like to do more sports. He started to include bicycle riding in his daily program, and he felt better after that.

A problem arises, naturally, when one part doesn't allow the other to express. Even this discovery can be positive, because change will surely follow. However, in this moment I am not presenting the ten questions so that you can modify something, but only to make you aware of how easy it is to be in contact with the man and the woman inside yourself.

Experiencing their contrasting qualities

I didn't tell you yet what you can expect to find, in terms of differences between the masculine and feminine energies.

The masculine energy, in its natural state, moves toward the outside. A man is outgoing. He likes expansion, he likes to stretch into bigger and bigger territories. He likes to touch, to outstretch the hands and have the fingertips meet something in that extension.

The feminine energy, on the contrary, by its very nature doesn't want to reach anywhere: for a woman, going to the moon has no significance! She moves toward the inner, she likes silence, she likes rest, she likes to simply be.

Let's take, for example, question five: if you work, which aspects are you doing? Generally the male will say, "organization, planning, solving practical problems." The female normally says, "relating with people, listening, finding solutions in an intuitive or nonrational way." This is when the male and female have the same work. It is not always so. Sometimes only half of you is doing the job, and the other half is not working. And sometimes when only one polarity is working, it doesn't like the job but does it simply for survival.

How you become partial to one

Returning to the difference between the masculine and the feminine, one loves the world, action, noise; the other loves intimacy, inaction, tranquility.

Which of these two we give more value depends to a large extent on our social conditioning. It can be determined by the culture or by the family.

Some cultures give importance to the irrational, and others to the rational, practical aspects of life. In the past, the peoples of India, Japan and China were surely of the first type, interested in beauty, grace, things which uplift the spirit—of course, today the polarity has changed and they are more interested in money and technology than before. Europe and America, at least in the past, always gave more value to material wealth, to conquering territories—witness the British colonies, for example. And exactly now there is a tendency toward change. Therefore, if one is born in a culture that appreciates art and music, literature and religion, he develops a point of view that is more feminine, and whatever is not symbolic, not connected to love or to the spirit, has less value for him. Another person, born in a culture which gives more value to money and technology, will tend to give little value to anything that is not utilitarian or concrete.

Also the family can determine the preference for one aspect over the other. If the father is the owner of a business, the son is influenced to follow this path. If the mother is a musician, the children are taught to appreciate things which create emotion and to consider them important.

This is just to show how it can happen that the two parts are not represented equally in your life. Perhaps you already noticed this when you responded to the questions. In question seven, one part could have responded that it has enough space, the other that it hasn't enough space.

There is another thing to consider. If one part has been dominant for a very long time, the second part can lose all hope for equal representation. And when its trust and self-respect go away, that weaker part becomes closed. In such a case we will no longer be able to see any spontaneous expression of that part. But this situation can be repaired.

The repair can happen naturally, without effort.

Usually, when we have the sensation that something has gone wrong, we try to put it right. We try! And the more we make effort, the more we become disturbed. This book is going to show you a completely new way to allow your male and female energies to take their rightful place in life. And when they do, it produces a sense of love and contentment inside yourself. The tension of incompleteness disappears, because your two parts are finally receiving from each other exactly what they always wanted.

CHAPTER 2

The Body's Energy Reveals the Characters

Perhaps it is a new idea for you that someone can get impressions or "see pictures" just by touching the physical body. It started happening to me spontaneously when I was quite young, perhaps twenty-three years old, and giving massages at the Esalen Institute in California. From the beginning, this psychic ability was not frightening to me. It was more of a shock for the client, I think, to have their body share with me information that only he or she could possibly know. For example, when I worked on one woman's back, I saw the image of her dog dying when she was a child. As I told her about it, she burst into tears for this animal; perhaps they were tears that had earlier been withheld, and so this memory had remained for many years locked in the subconscious.

After more and more experience working on bodies, I discovered that some parts of the body revealed pictures more readily than other parts. I started to pay careful attention, for example, to the hands, and also the heart area, both front and back. The vertebrae in the spine were a good source of information, particularly the tailbone. All of these places had a high concentration of nerve endings. I found myself poking into the small channels around the spinous processes of the spinal column, making contact with nerves as they carried impulses to and from the internal organs.

It was not common for me to speak during the massage. Of course, sometimes it happened that I heard a scream, or connected with a traumatic experience, and then I might tell the person immediately. But normally I continued to massage the person without talking, collecting images from every part of the body. By the end of the session I was able to formulate a comprehensive and coherent message to communicate to my client.

After some years of working this way, I began to be particularly fascinated by the pictures coming from the feet. If I just held one foot for a little while, the pictures began to roll one after the other, like a film where the plot thickens as one information is added to another. The first image was usually the body of a person; then I saw a place where they lived, and then I saw them making movements. It was like watching a cartoon artist create a character, and at the end he was flipping through frames to make a story.

I cannot say exactly when I understood for the first time that these images came from the male and female energies. I can only say that the more I gathered experience, the more I became sure that the right leg, and even more particularly the right foot, was showing me the masculine, and the left was showing me the feminine. At the time I thought it was interesting, but did not give it too much importance. To these two composite images, coming from the feet, I gave the same weight as any coming from the rest of the body.

Only many years later, after teaching counseling and working extensively with relationships, I started using an adaptation of Gestalt therapy technique to let the "characters" in the two legs talk to each other. (Later on I will tell you how it works.) From two chairs placed in front of each other, one character would describe the other, and vice versa. Without my intervention, the characters would describe down to fine details exactly the things I had seen when I "read" the feet. I was happy to have found a way to help the person make their own direct experience of the interior dialogue. It was much more meaningful than just having me tell them, as in an outsider's report, what was causing their problems.

How to receive pictures

Probably by now you are wondering, how is it possible to receive information psychically from the physical body of a person? It's not difficult, really. In case you want to experiment with reading energies, just follow the steps below. Once again you will need a friend to be your guinea pig, someone who is not your wife or husband—and girlfriends and boyfriends are included in that category! If you don't find a partner handy, or you simply want to skip this part, then advance directly to the next section.

The procedure:

· Ask your friend to lie down on their back with closed eyes. You place yourself near the chest, so if they are lying on a massage table, you stand at one side, or if they are on the floor or a bed, you seat yourself next to one arm, as close as you can.

· While the person relaxes a little, you also close your eyes and feel a kind of spaciousness in and around you. You spend a moment or two doing nothing. But even while you do nothing, you still notice that your body continues to expand and contract in breathing, your heart continues to beat, your nerves continue to register physical sensations. Even thoughts pass by—they come and go. And you simply become the empty space in which all these things happen. Many people experience this spaciousness as having a light grey color, similar to just before dawn. But sometimes it can also be dark grey or black.

- To feel this emptiness is to enter "in" yourself. And to keep contact with this feeling of "inner space," the most important thing is not to want any of the passing events to be different. You just presume that everything is fine as it is, and nothing needs to be changed.

- Gently move one hand over the heart of your partner. Keep your arm as relaxed as possible. The palm of your hand should arrive directly over the sternum, or breast-bone, about ten centimeters above the body. When the hand feels the energy of the person in this manner, you close your eyes again and imagine yourself watching a screen that is a little in front of your body. For me it is a blank screen, but some people say it is more like an empty sheet of paper, or like a whiteboard, or a blackboard, or like the night sky. You simply watch, waiting to see what might appear on this screen.

- If you don't immediately see pictures, just trust; not everyone is having visual perceptions. Sometimes, just watching the screen creates an atmosphere in which other things happen. You might hear words or sounds inaudible to others. You might experience sensations triggered by the other person's presence, or you might simply "know" something you were not aware of before. But normally, the impressions which come to you can best be described as pictures.

- As soon as you take your hand away from the chest of your partner, the picture will disappear. If you put your hand again over the heart, the image will come back—either this image or a similar one.

- Sometimes the question arises in you, "Is this image coming from me or from the other person?" There is a way to tell. When you watch the screen with your eyes closed, try to find the edges of the screen around the picture. If the edges are there, with empty space beyond, it means that you are detached, relaxed, and the picture is from the other. If you can't see the edges anymore, it means you have lost your objectivity and you have become involved: you are reacting to that which you feel.

· Now you can withdraw your hand. In your own rhythm, take leave of the chest and move nearer to the belly. When you have centered yourself again, let one hand go over the belly, about three fingers' width below the navel and 10 centimeters above the body. You are hovering over the second chakra, about which I will speak later. It's an important energy center and therefore a place from which you can receive images easily. Practice the same way you did with the heart.

· Now take your hand away from the belly, and sit relaxed near your partner, just resting in yourself.

The pictures you may have experienced are creations of your own mind, as it tries to interpret the energy coming in through your hand. Actually, the energy doesn't reach to the mind immediately, but it travels first into the feeling centers of your body, which are the heart, solar plexus, and abdomen. Once you feel something, you quite automatically ask the head to categorize the feeling, to give it a name. The head instantly sorts through all your past experience and perhaps comes up with a name which defines the feeling directly, a name like "fear" or "anger" or "joy." But more often, the feeling is complex, and then the mind will produce a picture in order to give you the message. You will be the only one able to decipher the message: just ask yourself, "What does this mean?" Don't ask your partner the significance of any picture, because they won't know!

Sometimes when you ask, "What does this mean," the mind gives you another picture. Ask again. If at this point the mind gives you a third picture, you simply look to see what the three pictures have in common.

Receiving these impressions, you are actually learning a new language. And as in all languages, some words are easier than others. Learn the easy words first—the ones connected to strong emotions, to the states of warmth and coldness, attraction and repulsion. After you've practiced a little, you will be able to recognize more complex states, but don't try to learn everything all at once.

Images from the feet

You practiced "reading" on the heart and the belly because these are the easiest places to use for learning. Now I would like to give you two examples of the kind of thing which can be "read" in the legs—at least, what kind of information I receive when I hold the feet and just rest inside myself.

The invisible woman

Marta is a tall and beautiful Italian who has just completed her studies for a doctorate in psychology. Recently she was attending a very tough psychological program in Holland where the work was "pushing," and on the last day she hurt her ankle so badly that she had to return to Italy for treatment and recovery.

Marta's reason for seeing me is that she is concerned for her feminine side. She feels her feminine part did not want to stay in Holland—hence the injury—and she has to learn how to recognize its needs and give it more space.

The reading:

Touching the left foot, at first I can't feel anything at all. It's like having in my hands a material object, but it's not living. There is no impression whatsoever, not even the darkness, or thickness, or heaviness that is usually present when the leg is closed. I wait a moment and slowly, slowly, some vague impressions start to arrive. This person is very, very fine, like a shadow or perhaps like a phantom. This person has chosen to become invisible. I can vaguely visualize a table where she is sitting next to a man who is very material—he's tearing meat from a bone with his teeth. And although she is in the next chair, she cannot be seen by him; the lines of her body are too ethereal.

This person generally remains silent. Although she can speak, she prefers not to because silence has more depth than talk.

Reading the right foot, I see a man about fifty years old. He is a bit heavy-set, with grey hair and a large mustache—all the details are clearly visible. He has on a fighting helmet, with the hair straggling out underneath, and around his waist is a wide metal belt with a sword on the side. His clothes are a kind of armor made of interlocking rings. I see him just coming back from work. It is about 10 o'clock at night. He enters an eating hall with a long trestle table; most everyone else has already finished eating and gone away. The room is rather dark, with a low peaked ceiling.

Next I see the man sitting at the rough wooden table with his plate of food and a tankard of ale. Even though there are not many people around, he is very talkative. His language is somewhat vulgar and the words are slurred; I wonder if he isn't a little bit drunk.

This man belongs to a military organization, and he is involved in some kind of reconnoitering or intelligence service about the movements of the enemy. He doesn't participate physically in battle, but he surveys the situation between his own team and the opposing one. This man has a self-important quality, a lot of pride in his abilities and his function—a conceit which in my opinion is unjustified.

That was the reading, but just so I don't leave you hanging I'll tell you what happened in this session. When the female side was expressing herself, I felt an elegance and refinement. She loved fineness, beauty, and grace. She was sensitive. She didn't like things that were gross and vulgar. So of course in the beginning she was sad, she was crying.

The male side liked strength, male strength. He said he didn't like women. He didn't like weakness. He liked hard, tough experiences. His eyes became quite narrow as he talked: "I'm very proud of myself. I like myself because I'm not afraid of anything, and because if there is a challenge I go for it, and I normally win. That's what is important for me—winning."

It was amazing to me that these two really did come closer together during the session. The male opened up—he *had* love under that false front, and also an ability not to take himself too seriously. The woman's attitude had been "don't touch me," but actually the session revealed a deeper fear that she "couldn't live without him." When she realized that she could live even better without him, she started to plan what she would like to do with her life. At that point the man realized that he had never seen *her*—her grace, her beauty—and he was stunned, he was crying.

So it was a good ending, after all.

The gambler

Aaron is a professional gambler, having lived off his winnings from horse races for almost twenty years. He came to me already two years ago, but now is returning because last winter he suddenly won quite a lot of money and he noticed that he didn't realize any of his dreams with it—that is, he didn't do what he had always planned to do when he was rich.

Left leg. The image is the same one I saw a couple of years ago.

The woman is wearing a full-length fur coat, cuddling up its flat collar against her neck. Underneath are the diamond earrings and low-cut dress that, according to the stereotype, you'd expect to see on a gambler's wife. The message is that she's longing for these sorts of fancy things. The difference between now and two years ago is that the outlines of the fur coat have less definition. They even vanish now and then. It's a sign that she could actually do without the fur coat now and still be perfectly fine.

So I guess it's okay that Aaron didn't realize his dreams for when he would be rich—they are no longer so dominant, and this is good.

Right leg. The image is of someone assiduously studying paperwork—the gambler not at the track but in another moment pouring over the facts and figures about the horses; or the stock market analyst checking every conceivable factor before he decides to act. This man, I conclude with surprise, is not a gambler at all but a person who refuses to accept the irrational. He believes there is an infallible way to figure out the results rationally, by sifting through reams of data. He is a "professional prediction analyst"! I will use this phrase later in the session to tease Aaron.

Resonance, a deep relaxation

I was reading the body's energy for many years before I happened to discover an information more important than the pictures. I will tell you now about it, but without proposing that you make a personal experiment this time.

While I was massaging, I became aware that some parts of the body—different ones from person to person—were producing a particular sensation on the inside of myself. It was not the same as seeing something on the screen. This was an effect upon the very center of myself. It is difficult to describe in words, but I became more alive inside. Sometimes this aliveness felt like an increase in love, sometimes like a feeling of expansion, and sometimes like the bubbles in champagne.

I came to recognize that these parts of the client's body were having a connection to my inner being. And regarding this connection, there were no longer two persons—the one out there and me in here—but we were one person. The aliveness in the other and the aliveness in me were a single phenomenon. This I felt as a "oneness" in myself that was richer than when I was alone. I used the word 'resonance' to describe this experience. I chose this word because the experience is similar to a phenomenon in music, when two tones are exactly the same so you hear only one sound, but it is richer because of the two instruments. In effect, I was having a kind of musical meeting with the client.

Now I have an explanation for this feeling. The life around us is like a flowing river and when we have a different goal than this river, we separate ourselves from it. When we just relax, and stop trying to have our own way, we are reunited with this river. The parts of the client's body which give me a sense of interior expansion are harmoniously connected to this river of life; they are deeply relaxed. Which is to say, these parts of the body are psychologically and spiritually healthy.

Unfortunately, it's not so very easy to find in people's bodies this quality of presence that brightens my own inner being. But when I find it in someone I can assume that, at least regarding one aspect of life, this person has no problem. This part of the body I know is functioning well.

What do I mean when I say it functions well? It depends on where I find resonance. If I find it in the heart, it means that the person knows what love is and emanates love simply by breathing!

If I find resonance at the solar plexus, it means that when this person tells other people what to do, the others are glad to cooperate.

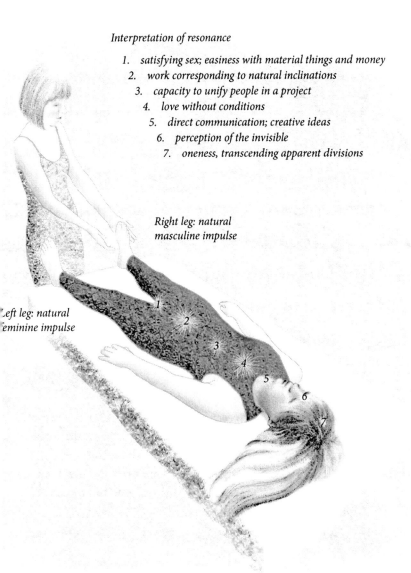

Interpretation of resonance

1. satisfying sex; easiness with material things and money
2. work corresponding to natural inclinations
3. capacity to unify people in a project
4. love without conditions
5. direct communication; creative ideas
6. perception of the invisible
7. oneness, transcending apparent divisions

Right leg: natural
masculine impulse

Left leg: natural
feminine impulse

When a chakra is resonant, it indicates an availability to the river of life. That is,
responses are ever-changing, appropriate to new circumstances. This part of the body
is not tied to the past, not repeating what is old. It is fluid and continuously fresh.

This person is a natural leader. When I find resonance in the belly, it means that the work this person does corresponds to his or her natural inclinations. More precisely, resonance in the belly tells me that the person is in the right place at the right time—brought there by relaxation.

Once I had understood that resonance is a capacity to "let go" to the river, I started to look for it in the major energy centers of the body. These are called *chakras*, discovered a long time ago in India to be places where energy is more concentrated. According to the sages of the past, there are seven of them situated between the base of the pelvis and the top of the head, but also some smaller energy centers in the hands and the feet.

Gradually I started to check these energy centers in my client before the start of my session. With eyes closed, I looked "out" at the screen to find the images, and I looked "in" at my meditation space to find the resonance. In this way, it was possible for me to discern in less than ten minutes whether the person was psychologically and spiritually healthy. Also, it was possible to know in which direction the person should proceed in order to have more well-being.

Once this clarity could be reached so quickly, I had lots of time left to help the client make his own direct experience of the truth, instead of just listening to my words. At this point I stopped using the medium of massage and started to develop verbal devices which allowed the person to see what I had seen, just by looking within himself.

I call this new method "Star Sapphire," naming it after the sapphire gemstone which looks quite undistinguished on the surface, but when you hold it in a certain light, it reveals a six-pointed star. For me, people are like that—they carry inside themselves an unexpected luminosity. My job is simply to hold a mirror at the right angle so that they can have a glimpse of their own untarnished inner glow.

CHAPTER 3

The Contrast between Personality and Being

A s I just told you, there is information coming from the body that is more important than images, something I call *resonance*. This means that the essence of the person is touching the same essence in me. There's a contact, and a feeling of being one.

The idea should not be so strange to you. Sometimes it happens the same way in life, too, that with some people you don't feel any connection but with others you feel yourself naturally more full of joy.

I am going to be discussing why some parts of the body have resonance and others don't, but you can understand that this is an extension of the more general concept that some people have resonance and others don't. To begin my explanation, I need to go first in another direction.

Trust and fear: two different viewpoints

I have to talk for a moment about parents and children. Many parents consider a child to be a blank page, a "tabula rasa." They believe that if they don't write something on this blank page, the child will not know what to do in life. Or even worse, the child will end up doing nothing at all. And so they perceive it as their duty to mold him, to instruct him, and to indicate what things are to be done and how they should be done. Any child treated like this will tend to fear his natural impulses, especially when they conflict with the parents' directives. He will always have a doubt inside himself: "Is what I feel right or wrong?"

There is another type of parents, or if you prefer, there is another way to educate a child. And that is to teach self-trust. Self-trust arises from the viewpoint that everyone is born as part of a vast, fluctuating energy network, similar to a river. If you just rest in it, this river will carry you into positive new experiences. It will inspire you to take unique and creative actions—things that can't be decided ahead of time but that arise in the moment like waves. If a child is brought up by parents who comprehend this, he will not produce any division inside himself; there will be no conflict between what he is and what he should be.

The two views of life are unavoidably in contradiction with each other. One is based on fear, the other is based on trust. With the first point of view, the person can never relax; he always has to control to make sure that things go well. With the second point of view, the person can allow relaxation because he knows, deep down, that everything will surely go well. Therefore, the second vision creates a general relaxation in the body, while the first creates a general contraction.

The majority of people in the world live with the "fear" attitude, and so they are tense. A smaller minority of people carry the "trust" attitude. Perhaps one attitude is not necessarily more right than the other, but certainly one is more easy-going and more fun than the other. And the good news is that it is possible to choose the relaxing approach to life as an adult, even if your parents don't share it. Meditation is a way to experience the "trust" view, and I will tell you what I mean in the next chapter.

For now, the point is that when you trust life, you relax. It is this relaxation that produces resonance. Trust is a decision on your part not to fix ahead of time what you will do, not to prepare, not to plan, simply to meet the events of the moment and flow naturally with them. And then it is life that molds you, that continually gives you new forms, so that you have no fixed shape or posture in particular. In fact, you will never be able to know who you are if you expect to find a fixed form: you are a little river connected to a much bigger river that is ever-changing.

When I find resonance in a body, it indicates to me that the person knows what it means to "let go" to this river. And when the resonance is coming from a particular part of the body, the images that I am able to see there—the "pictures" that I told you about in the last chapter—start to become more faded, the outlines become less sharp. This is because they represent fixed forms, identities that the person had in the past, and perhaps still has to some degree, but now they are no longer strong. And if resonance grows more and more, in this part of the body the pictures will disappear altogether; when I look for them, I won't see anything.

Personality is effort; being is no-effort

Perhaps you are asking, if resonance is created by relaxation, why doesn't everybody have it? The answer is that we are not used to relaxation, we are used to effort. Everybody teaches us to have goals and to try hard to reach them—particularly our parents. They instill in us many ambitions: for example, to be the first in the class, to become a professor or a famous scientist. Or, if they don't have specific requests, they assume that whatever we do has to be perfect and that we should be successful at it.

These things require effort, much effort. Our muscles become chronically contracted because of this effort, and after a certain time we start to experience this tension in the body as our "self."

In fact, the more we make effort the more intensely we feel this self, and we start to believe it is who we *are*. But actually this solid, substantial feeling, based on tension, has nothing to do with who we really are. It is only the personality.

Personality is the sum of all our desires to become someone or something. These can be desires that we absorb from other people or our own desires, it makes not much difference because the effort to fulfill them creates personality. Generally people are proud of what they have achieved by effort. You can hear it in the voice of someone who says, "I'm a doctor," or " I'm a professor." But the personality is actually the thing that keeps us separate from others. It's like a shell that surrounds the seed of life and protects it. The funny thing is that many persons walk around enclosed in their shells, even showing off their shells, without realizing that they are guardians of something much more precious.

We know how to live making effort, we have become certain that we can earn enough money to survive, and so the proposal to relax, to not make effort, is a little unnerving. The question immediately comes up, "What will happen if I relax? How will I be able to survive?" Well, I won't answer this question in one sentence, but later on in this book some chapters should inspire you to answer it yourself.

Instead, right now I can suggest a name for that which is the opposite of personality: the *being*. Your being is simply there when you don't make effort. Sometimes you feel it unexpectedly while you are listening to music, or lying on a beach, or driving your car without any need to hurry. You feel well, you have no worries or preoccupations, you are content—it is a contentment that has no particular outside cause.

Sometimes you feel your being when you are quiet, doing nothing. But also you can feel it when you are full-on in activity, while dancing in a discotheque or while holding a conference about your work. The similarity in all cases is that you feel at ease, natural.

And you feel yourself happy in the activity, or non-activity.

There is something that obstructs the ongoing state of naturalness in us. Before, I said that it was ambition, the search to continually reach objectives. But if you look deeper you will notice inside yourself a mechanism called "mind," whose job is to fabricate the objectives. It continually makes pictures of things that don't exist yet. With these objectives, the mind feels "full."

I used to think that desire was the reason that we go away from our being. But later I understood that desire is a secondary phenomenon. The real reason is the fear of emptiness. People cannot tolerate having such a void inside, hence they create objectives to have something with which to occupy themselves: better this than nothing!

The black hole of desire

I'll give you an example of a desire. Your husband is at work, and you don't know when he'll come home but you hope it's early. You make an image in your head that he will return at 8:00 pm, or at the latest 9:00 pm, but not midnight. The idea is attractive, you watch it as if you were seeing a film, and it's pleasant. But when after some moments you remember that this is a film, created only by you, you sigh with a recognition of the truth that you don't know if he'll be home before or after midnight.

Desires are born of the dream-like fantasy that things might be different than they are. I'll give you another example, analyzing an action that you do regularly. You go into your room, you take off your sweater and leave it on a chair. An hour later you return to your room and, noticing the sweater, you have the desire to put the sweater away in the closet. Your mind makes a picture of the sweater already in its place in the closet, folded on top of a pile of other sweaters.

I would like you to put your attention on that exact moment

when there is a contrast between where the sweater really is—on the chair—and the image in your mind, showing the sweater already in another place. It's exactly at this moment that you have to ask if you really want to do the actions necessary to put it in its new place. If you don't feel any joy in doing it, then abandon the desire. But many people don't take care of what they feel, they just immediately implement the idea they have in their mind, as if it were a duty. And if you stop them in the middle of the operation and don't permit the satisfaction of their desire, you will see an interesting fact: they didn't get any fulfillment from what they have done up to the moment of stopping—that is, prior to actually placing the sweater in the closet.

This example serves to show you that when we live in desires, the only moment of fulfillment is usually at the end of the process, at its completion. If in realizing a certain desire it takes one year, for example to acquire a house, the many moments along the way seem dry; only the moment of acquisition makes you feel any joy.

Ironically, the joy doesn't last very long and immediately another desire arrives. Having bought the house, you want to renovate it, and then you decide that it is missing a fireplace, and when you've had that constructed, you notice that sparks from the fireplace are damaging the wooden floor, and if you don't take care of it… There's always something that has yet to be put right, because the mind has this habit of continually producing ideas of perfection in contrast to the reality.

And it's always like that. We are habituated to a type of sufferance caused by the contrast between that which we want and expect, and the fact that we don't have it yet. And we are constantly focused on the thing that is missing. In this way, the mind has become too important—its ideas of a perfect future are making us feel constantly impoverished.

That which we have is never enough. For example, you have a

girlfriend but she's not as pretty as you hoped, she talks too much and her voice gets on your nerves. And besides, she complains about your bad habits. You forget to be happy that you *have* a girlfriend; there are other men who don't have one, and they would like to be in your shoes!

There are many things to notice about desire, about the process of desiring. One is that it takes you into the future and you lose contact with the present experience. Another thing is that you start to become cunning, thinking always about what could be the best strategy for satisfying your desire. And third, desire by its very nature requires effort. We are so accustomed to making effort that we don't even realize that there could be another way.

I've spoken to you about desires like getting a house, but there are more profound desires than this: for example, the desire to live. The wish to stay alive is so familiar that you might not think it should be classified as a desire. But most people are not relaxed on the subject of survival. They are fighting for it. And behind every struggle there is desire.

Another deep yearning is for physical contact, for sex. A female person is very much attracted to a male person and vice versa. Men and women meet, but what they dreamed would happen when they come together never happens. They want to be fulfilled by each other, but instead of fulfillment they find frustration. Why? The reason is that neither has anything to give, neither of the two has any love, and they each expect to receive something from the other. As if each were a baby bird with a mouth much bigger than the body, holding it wide open to be fed. The baby bird is my favorite symbol for desire, where the fulfillment is always in the future and in the present there is only emptiness.

I will leave my favorite image now and change to another metaphor in order to better describe the relationship between men and women. Think of a woman with this emptiness inside that I've been speaking about, and imagine that she is a vacuum cleaner. If a man, another vacuum cleaner, approaches her, the hoses of the two vacuum cleaners "stick" together in suction. Of course, then it is quite difficult to separate them. Paradoxically, in spite of their nearness neither the woman nor the man experiences a real meeting; they continue to feel only need, never fulfillment. Most of our relationships are like that.

Very often it happens that one part can't stand the pull, so it tries to fight the desire of the other. With great effort, it becomes separate.

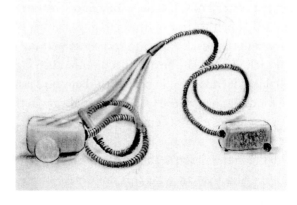

But this "no" is another type of desire, the desire to be alone. One person desires to be in a couple, the other desires to be alone, and the desiring holds them together. In fact, if the one who is longing and asking "please give me" were ever to leave the one that is saying "no," the second would find another partner who has need, to which he (or she) can then say no... enacting the drama again and again.

There is a third possibility but it is not so familiar. To realize it, one of the two persons has to undergo an energetic transformation. One of the two partners has to search within himself or herself, has to discover inside a flow that gives nourishment. If this flow starts to determine the actions in life, the energy moves in a contrary way to the vacuum cleaner: instead of sucking things in from outside, something is created on the inside and then sent outwards, much like the sun emanates warmth from its center.

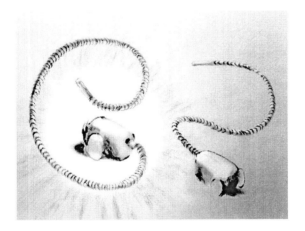

The other person, who still has the energy of a vacuum cleaner, will be surprised. He will remember the sensation that he was used to when he was glued to the other by suction—even though he was receiving nothing. So in the beginning, he feels a loss. But with a little attention, he will realize that even though he has "lost" the object of his desire, he feels better; he feels himself surrounded by a more nourishing atmosphere than before.

One of the aims of this book is to show how to realize this energy transformation.

I'm going to share with you some bits of a session I had with Allison, where I was proposing to her exactly this direction. Below you won't see a whole session, but only the diagnosis, because it fits with the present topic. You will notice that I'm not asking the weaker side, in this case the male side, to change in any way. I don't even mention him. It is part of the Star Sapphire concept to put the pressure for growth on the stronger side, the side which can commit itself to change and can enjoy the challenge of self-reliance.

The three levels of love

Allison comes to me more out of curiosity than for any serious motivation. She is married, and when I ask her if she is happy in the relationship she says, "Yes and no—50% yes and 50% no."

During the resonance check of the chakras, I see a luminous and loving energy in the left leg, but it is not resonant. I see an image of her looking out to get love, expectantly, like a small child. When she doesn't get it, she withdraws into the shadows but she doesn't stop hoping; maybe in a later moment she will try again.

The right leg is heavy when I lift it to hold the foot. The energy is flat, boring, with no resonance. The inner man is closed but not hostile—I would say rather total in his decision to be closed.

Allison's first chakra is at least a little juicy, more alive than the legs below, the second also, and in these I feel her willingness to find the path. Her third chakra is closed, having the same quality as the masculine leg. In chakra four, the energy is like the feminine leg. I find lots of light and warmth that is very close to resonance but not the same. Some kind of grounding in love is missing, but just a slight "click" is needed for it to happen. Chakra five is closed, and the other two in the head are not lived in yet.

I have a few things to say to Allison that might help her find the right track:

"When I hold your left foot, which in my work represents the feminine aspect of the body, I find it loving but with a type of love that waits for somebody else to give love back. Because of this expectation, the other person isn't free to love you or not. You don't leave the other person any space. It's a common thing, almost everybody knows this type of love that is a bargain, 'I give you, and you give me...'

"Actually there are three different levels of love. The first is sexual love, in which both the persons take something from each other. The second comes from the heart, but it is a bargain—this is the kind you know. Then there's the third, which happens when you have so much love that it no longer depends on what the other does. It showers on everyone, those who deserve it and those who don't. For this level of love, you have to discover a source within yourself where you don't need anything from the other for love to be complete.

"Why do people get stuck at this level of 'I love you—would you please love me back'? It happens because we have developed a false sense of self. The real self is actually full of love; the false self continuously desires and, because of thinking there is never enough, it always hankers for more and more. If you intend to find the real self, the first step is to accept that this 'I' is a false self, and that you don't know the real one yet.

"Allison, I congratulate you for having a feminine side that is very loving. But this love is still limited by the sense of 'I'. At the moment, this 'I' is waiting for somebody to love you. And sometimes you are disappointed—then in that shock, in that disappointment, you pull back. You haven't yet chosen to go 'in'; you are simply waiting for the next opportunity to ask."

I felt that Allison needed only one thing: meditation. I explained to her that meditation is a moment in which, without any distraction from outside, you relax in observing yourself. But it's different than the kind of relaxing we do on weekends when we ignore or avoid situations. Actually, we are in a kind of sleep state most of the time. We want to do our work almost sleeping, and then on the weekends we want to sleep some more! Meditation is the opposite: it is relaxation and alertness combined. It is a kind of waking up to how things are in reality.

In Allison's case, we did a guided meditation together and in this way she was able to have her first taste.

CHAPTER 4

What is Meditation

The habits that many of us imbibed from parents and from the society don't take us inward, toward the center of ourselves, but rather in an outward direction. Our parents have always told us to look for attractive things in the world, to acquire them and to attach ourselves to them. In short, they taught us to desire.

However, no one ever told us a very important thing: that a life built on desire is dangerous. Whatever you manage to get, in fact, can be taken away. If you think to possess persons, like a wife or children, these too can leave you by their own volition. In that moment you will experience the hole that you have filled up by having possessions. I want to say that this style of life actually hides the fear of loss. And it hides the fear of death—where you lose everything.

When we totally comprehend this situation, or when the life has torn away from us all that we considered important, we start to be interested in finding a fullness that is not dependent on possessing someone or something outside. This fullness exists, but as I said before it requires that we undergo a kind of energetic transformation.

Imagine yourself having a desire that takes only five minutes to fulfill: the desire to buy a new CD. You step out from your apartment, close the door, walk one block to the music shop, ask there for what you want, extract your wallet to pay, and you leave with the CD in your hands. In this whole process you waited for one particular moment: possessing the CD. This was the moment of maximum satisfaction. Most probably you didn't have the same joy in the moments when you closed the door to your house, when you turned the key, when you descended the stairs, when you walked on the street. Out of 1000 moments, you had only one good one. The other 999 were spent thinking of the one good moment in the future, disconnected from your present reality of moving your body from the house to the shop, moment by moment.

Observing that which is, before you try to change it

The secret to finding a fullness within yourself is to let go of thoughts and to enter in contact with that which is actually happening in the moment. If you are able to do this, it changes the quality of your actions—even purchasing a CD. You will leave your apartment in a different way. As you turn the key in the lock, you will notice if the rhythm with which you do it comes from relaxation and feels good to you, or if the rhythm causes tension. And the same is true about walking on the street. You will be able to notice if you are taking a step in a rush to reach to the future goal or if the rhythm is joyous and puts you in a good mood.

I said "if" you are able to do it, because many people are not able to come out of the mind, not even for a single moment. They occupy themselves with a million things to do, and it has been a habit for such a long time that they no longer have control over when to use the mind and when to let it rest. I say this because the mind is not always necessary: it is useful for programming the future, but it is absolutely useless for contacting the present. For that we need a method which brings us to the present, and this method is called meditation.

Many people think that meditation means you sit immobile with the legs crossed, the spine straight, and the eyes closed. At least that is what I thought when I started. Actually I'm not against this idea, because what happened to me after five times of sitting this way was certainly a taste of meditation. But now I know that meditation can happen in any sort of position and with any type of movement: the Buddha has no fixed posture!

For the modern man it is much better to use meditations that start with phases of movement, because if you are total in movement, the silence which follows afterwards will be more alive and more pleasurable. Moreover, if in the moving phase you have already been experiencing a flowing energy which is not preprogrammed by the mind, when you stop, this no-thought state continues and you just add to it no-movement. In this way you easily get familiar with the absence of thought and movement, and you discover that the "space" you find then is not really empty at all, but full of a very nice feeling which cannot be described in words.

There are hundreds of techniques for meditation, but all of them have the same essence: the attitude of not trying to make this moment different than it is. You simply look at that which is being born exactly now, which can be a feeling or a thought or a movement; you observe its facticity, and don't try to change it. I often tell myself, as a reminder, "Keep your hands off!"

It takes a certain practice to succeed at not interfering with what comes into your awareness. I give you an example of how it can go. If you feel a scream inside you, normally you judge it and repress it. Instead, try to see the two things, the physical impulse and the thought (which is your judgment); observe them and let them exist together. Literally, you are doing nothing. If the impulse to scream becomes more strong and you are in a place where you can permit it, then let the body scream, but remain still a witness, without being for or against the event.

After a bit of practice in this direction, you will make a discovery. The watcher itself is calm even when the thing you are watching has a certain intensity. You can watch fear, and the watcher doesn't feel any fear; you can watch boredom, and the watcher doesn't feel bored. The watcher is disidentified from the thing it is watching. You are excited because a desire has been fulfilled, but the watcher isn't. You are depressed because a desire has been thwarted, but the watcher is not depressed. The watcher remains absolutely the same through the ups and downs of life: it is never identified.

Relaxation and trust in natural impulses

When observing without interfering in that which happens becomes a habit, your whole body-mind system relaxes deeply. "Doing" has created tension, and the "non-doing" I've been speaking about releases tension. It's like discovering that there is no better moment than now, and you live it without effort.

You might think that if you practice this, the events in your life will become more calm. It is not the case. As relaxation goes deeper, repressed impulses start to come to the surface. The more you abandon the decision of what you want to watch, the more likely it is that you will see things you don't like about yourself, things that have been hidden on purpose in the past. This is why after a short time you could stop meditating. But if you continue, with trust, you can meet every "shady" part of yourself with a welcoming attitude, and this acceptance is healing. Not only that. If in the beginning you also encounter regularly a kind of darkness, with time this darkness thins out and your natural impulses become more clear and strong. I want to tell you that while the witness is always calm, with meditation your life becomes more vital, more active, more wild. And often it starts to go quite contrary to what other people are expecting of you. So, anything but calm!

What follows is a guided meditation which I usually lead personally in groups. Naturally it is supposed to be experienced with your eyes closed; ideally you would first listen and then do, in place of reading. But if this is not possible, read it by yourself, slowly, and use it to enter the meditative state.

A guided meditation

For this experiment, you can stand with the legs slightly apart. Close your eyes and take a few breaths to come in contact with your body. Then move your weight gently over one leg and for a moment let the other one be empty. If you relax, the impulse to move to the opposite side will happen by itself, and you follow it. The first leg, in its turn, becomes empty.

In the beginning, holding the weight on just one leg feels fresh and pleasant, but very soon it becomes a burden, and you naturally transfer it to the other leg. Go on permitting this movement from one side to the other.

While practicing this, observe exactly which leg has the weight now. The sensation in that foot will be more intense because the weight is making a pressure, the sole of the foot is more squashed than before, the muscles are alert to make sure you don't fall over. But none of these things takes effort. The leg was born for this type of activity, the muscles know how to hold the body upright—it's their job.

Each time you move, you'll notice small differences in the experience of the weight arriving over one leg. One time the weight goes more on the heel, the next time the pelvis rotates by itself, another time the knee bends. You simply continue to allow the shifting from side to side, noticing surprises.

If you let the legs have even more freedom, they start to do other things, and you watch. Maybe the feet don't remain parallel, one points itself in a new direction, and the other, coming back to the floor, also finds a new position. Maybe you make a strange and funny walk, in which you move sometimes one way, sometimes another, sometimes in a circle. The feet decide.

While you do this, always be perfectly ready to say which leg has the weight.

Let yourself divide the walking into smaller pieces, where each step is an event in itself. With careful observation, you will see that each step has a beginning, a middle, and an end. The beginning is when the foot makes contact with the ground. When the pressure of the weight on the foot becomes strong, that's the middle. And when the weight is released, and the foot loses contact with the ground, you've come to the end. In the case of a single step, the changes are very quick. But notice that you can anyway feel the three distinct moments.

Now observe the process of only one foot. When the step begins, you are watching; when the step is in its fullest expression, you are watching; and when the action finishes, you are watching. And when the foot is in the air and there's no longer any event—at least for this foot—you are still watching. In fact the watcher never changes, while the event is born, flourishes, and dies.

The event is the outer aspect of meditation and the silent acceptance is the inner aspect of meditation. Some people mistakenly think that only the inner aspect has importance, but in reality, the inner doesn't have value without the outer, which gives color, taste, and ecstasy to the inner silence. And the inner gives an invisible profundity to the outer event. You can imagine the ocean, which on the surface has waves but in the depths nothing moves.

I ask you to feel again both feet, making steps one after the other. They know what to do, sometimes they turn, sometimes they slide on the ground, sometimes they are lazy, sometimes playful, you simply let them choose their place, their rhythm, and you rest in the movement between the two.

The step of one foot dies in the same moment that another step is born, and the feet are not worried. One surrenders to the other knowing that the death of one step is not a problem but a time of regeneration. The first leg knows that the second leg is a friend, and vice versa. Their reciprocal friendship creates a loving flow between them, and you simply observe this, without doing anything.

From this example you can see there exists a strong connection between relaxation and trust. If you don't have trust in how a foot is moving itself, you can't relax with its choice. The choice of the feet to move backwards, for example, isn't mental: we say that it is "no-mind" or "beyond the mind," or "coming from natural impulse."

Practicing this meditation you will trust in your feet without even noticing it, and you will relax in the fact that they cannot make any wrong step. A meditator, in a certain sense, abandons every idea about things right or wrong. And, if he is fortunate, he manages to not have any preconceived idea about how he will behave—he accepts whatever arises from his interior. What really counts is his interest in the truth inside: without this, at the first conflict between his own truth and the social conventions, he might abandon himself in order to stay connected with the society.

I'm not saying that you should become a disturbance to other people. A meditator can be prudent: if he notices that he's angry while in the middle of a crowd, he doesn't need to choose that very moment to express his anger. He can do it later, in his own room, using a meditation in which the music encourages catharsis. He can jump, shout, cry, and express all his rage against the others, knowing very well that he is the only one responsible for his feeling, the others are not the reason for it. This is exactly the opposite of what happens normally in daily life, when every occasion is great for putting out one's rage, for example, on the guy who blocks the street and creates a traffic jam.

You can be conscious of what emerges from inside without judging it as bad or wrong. If it's a question of anger, I don't want to say that you should repress it—but first of all you have to see it, acknowledge it. The other person is giving you an opportunity to be in contact with this part of yourself. Alone, or in a meditation together with others, you can permit this feeling to flow. You will discover that underneath anger there is sadness and beneath this, love. And so, if you succeed in being total in expressing the so-called negative feelings in an appropriate situation, you will often experience that the original source of these emotions is innocent.

Different meditations for the masculine and the feminine sides

The essence of meditation is one, but there are many techniques that can bring you into deeper contact with yourself. I have discovered, after many years of experimentation, that some of these techniques are more helpful for the feminine and others give more dignity and strength to the masculine.

My first experiences were with Vipassana meditation, which is the type where you sit cross-legged, in silence, and observe the breath. Certainly you observe more than just the breath, because the mind continues to distract you. But I chose a meditation without movement or sound, in which the implicit objective was that "actions"—that is, the events—should be reduced to zero.

This sort of experience can be blissful for the female; she can relax into herself. The feminine, as I have said, is more interested in things invisible, and I am one of that type. I have always been attracted to having the eyes closed, to feeling the space inside the body as an emptiness, and to having the quality of love that I can meet while resting in myself.

Many years later I discovered that my inner man had never participated in Vipassana, and I discovered it in a strange way. One day in a meditation I could not manage to keep my eyes closed. When I tried, they opened wide, immediately. And I heard my inner man saying to me, "If I close my eyes, I lose myself, and the female takes all the space."

After this I started to create meditations in which my inner man could be content. For example, one of my favorites is to stand upright, with the legs shoulder-width apart, and do a certain breathing where the pelvis moves backward when I breathe in and forward when I breathe out. At the same time, when I breathe in the eyes open wide, looking at the ceiling, and when I breathe out, the eyes become more closed until I am looking at the ground. The essence of the meditation is the same as Vipassana in the sense that one observes what happens during breathing, without changing anything. But with this much movement in the pelvis and the eyes, my male has fun, while in normal Vipassana he is bored and doesn't participate.

This was how I happened to discover that the male and female sides have preferences even in meditation. Women like meditations in which the eyes are closed, the movements are delicate and non-muscular, and the sounds don't have any purpose—like the kind that come from babies. Men, on the other hand, like physicality, loud sounds, and forceful actions, as if to maintain a contact with the external world. The best type of meditation has phases for both. But it's also true that in some moments of life one has more need for a female type of meditation or for a male type, to give support to one part, and vice versa.

A breath meditation for both

Once more I propose to you a meditation where you stand up, with your feet parallel and shoulder-width apart. The knees are relaxed—neither stiffly straight nor bent, but just easy.

Take a nice breath and feel it in the belly. When the belly receives the air, allow the sacrum—the flat part of the lower spine—to be pushed backward. And when the air goes out, the sacrum falls again more forward. Breathing in this way, you notice that the pelvis is moving first backward and then forward with each inhalation and exhalation.

The knees change position by themselves, adjusting to the change of weight. They know what to do to keep the body upright, even when five kilos are being displaced forward and backward during the breathing. Permit yourself to feel the legs while you breathe, and let yourself be surprised by how the muscles know exactly when to contract and relax in support of the breath.

Now feel your feet. When you breathe into the pelvis and it moves backward, its weight goes over the heels. As soon as you exhale, the weight moves from the heels to the toes. Feel your feet involved in this miracle, to remain standing in an erect position and breathing at the same time. This is love coming from the legs, even if they are not trying to love. They are just being natural.

Now I ask you to breathe more fully, so that you can feel first the belly and then the chest. When you exhale, the air leaves the chest and it becomes smaller, the length of the spine is reduced, the sacrum comes down and under. I would like you to feel this breath as having four parts: the beginning, the peak, the decline, and the end. Breathe deeply a few times, and see if you manage to take the breath to the limit of each of these four stages.

The first two quarters of the breath are masculine; inhalation is masculine. Notice how you feel in the first part, when the impulse arrives and you don't know from where. All of a sudden there is a push toward expansion, and you follow it. It feels very pleasant.

In the second stage, the original impulse is extended to its limit—in this case, the body simply cannot become bigger. The ribs have arrived at the maximum distance from each other, the sternum is elevated as much as possible, and the shoulders can't lift more than that. The masculine energy has this wish to go as far as it can, until it meets a barrier. It pours itself into a form (in this case, the body), makes this form taut, makes the outlines more specific, makes the limits clear, but also it feels constrained by the form and always wants to go further.

When you begin the third part of the breath, the feminine becomes active. At first she seems to be taking something away from the masculine. Before, the periphery of the body was stretched taut. Now that this energy is reduced, there is less pressure and the form begins to disappear. For the feminine, this is better. She doesn't like the pressure nor the form. She doesn't like the confrontation with a barrier and the fight to get a bigger space. And so she pulls you out of this conflict, which doesn't interest her, and goes more "backward" or "downward" into herself.

The third and fourth stages of the breath are feminine. In the third, the feminine is relieved of tension and in the fourth she takes this direction to its extreme, which is a sort of death. You arrive at the bottom of the exhalation, and for one fraction of a second there is nothing left except emptiness. If this emptiness were to continue forever it would be boring. But from some unknown corner, we don't know from where, the male part starts to do his thing again, revitalized by his period of inactivity.

Carry on with breathing, and as you watch these four quarters, find out which part you like best. It will also tell you something about your life right now—for example, which stage of a work project will make you feel good.

Also notice which phase of the breath you don't want to feel. For some people it's the peak, for others it's the death. For still others, the relaxation at the end of the breath is so pleasant that each new inhalation is a disturbance, and they don't want it to come.

Now try one more thing. Breathe in, and when the pelvis goes backward and the chest is stretched, permit your eyes to open with the rest of the body. When you breathe out, permit the eyes to close, while the body moves toward the absence of form. Continue to breathe, watching what happens to your eyes. Probably at the maximum of the inspiration, they see clearly the colors, the shapes of the surrounding objects, and when you exhale there is less interest in external things, the vision is more diffused.

The observer notices that in one moment there is an impression of color on the outside, and in the next moment, the color has disappeared. But the observer stays the same, always the same. The observer feels the pelvis go backward on the inhale and forward on the exhale, The observer is always there, when you don't try to do something but simply notice that the masculine energy makes the body more big and then the feminine energy makes it more small. The masculine energy brings the breath in, and the feminine releases it.

There's nothing you have to do, only to observe the dance between the two. You are the mystery that happens between them. You are love. Close your eyes and feel the atmosphere that these two polarities have created, simply because each one was true to itself.

CHAPTER 5

Work, Relationship, and Meditation: three interdependent areas

On the surface it's difficult to see how what you do in bed at night with your girlfriend has anything to do with your activities at work. It's difficult to see how crossing the city in a taxi, dodging the rush-hour traffic, can have anything to do with the moments in which you are sitting in meditation with your eyes closed in a silent room. In fact there's a connection, hidden but very important, between the success you have at your job, your ability to be in harmony with your partner, and your access to the inner silence called meditation.

To understand this connection, we have to return to the concept of resonance. When I tune in to the resonance in someone's body, I perceive it as a kind of light—actually I don't see this light as an object, but rather I notice the light inside myself growing bigger. As I said before, if a certain part of the person's body has resonance it means that this part is in a condition of relaxation, having no plans for what is going to happen next. It is available for the moments to be shaped by the larger forces of existence.

It's difficult to find words for this state. Some people call it "no-mind," "absence of ego," "no-I", and some others label it "surrendering to existence," "letting go." For me, the best description is to say that this part of the body has trust. There is trust that whatever the future brings will have love in it, and so one doesn't need to worry. One has only to relax, and the right things will happen in a natural way.

The truth about your job? You'll find it in the legs

At the end of chapter two, I presented a resonance chart to show what happens as various parts of the body relax in this way. Now I want to say something more specific regarding the legs and feet.

When there is resonance in the feet, it indicates an attunement with natural impulse—feminine impulses come from the left foot, masculine from the right. These impulses, obviously, flow upward, where they can be put into action by the rest of the body. Sometimes they can be blocked along the pathway through the legs, but this is rare. Usually, if a true impulse is generated by one foot, it reaches to the first chakra. And if true impulses are being generated by both feet, they join each other in the first chakra. It is like there are two separate rivers originating in the feet, and when they reach the base of the spine they merge to form one river that then continues upward to the top of the head.

Consider just one of these legs alone, for a moment. Let's take, as an example, the right leg which is the inner man. If this leg presents resonance, the person—at least in his male aspect—is for sure involved in work that is suitable for him because his activity arises from relaxation. And for this person it will be easy to earn money by means of a job that is not tiring.

I'm saying this to explain that natural impulses on one side of the body, in this case the masculine, are the ground for successful work, or perhaps I should say joyful responsibility in work. And sometimes I use a short form—for which I ask your indulgence—saying

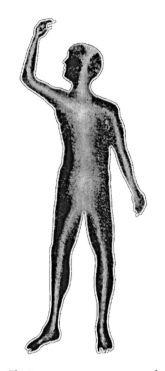

The inner partners are separate from the feet to the pelvis, and they join each other in chakra one.

that the "leg has a job," when of course it is actually the whole person who has an occupation.

All the same things apply to the female as well, although her inclinations are very different than the male's.

Very often, the male and female sides participate in the same job. For example if a person is a director of personnel, his (or her) male side can be the part that decides how to cut expenses, and the female side can be the part which feels the qualities of employees and tries to find the right place for them in the company.

Sometimes the two sides of a person find expression in completely different jobs. I know of one professor of psychology whose male side is gifted in administration. He is in process of starting a new university, taking care of the bureaucratic arrangements and asking for various permissions. And while he does that, the female side is writing a book about the artist El Greco and playing music in a professional band.

But it doesn't make any difference whether you have the two expressions within the same job or two different jobs; the important thing is that these expressions come from a natural source, from your relaxation, from the "no-I." It also doesn't make a difference if one part earns money and the other doesn't; what matters is the feeling of being creative in a way that has meaning and significance for you.

How the three areas are linked to one another

Up to now, I've been speaking about natural impulses and the work that arises from a leg which has resonance. But resonance also furnishes another piece of information: the state of meditation is present in this leg. As I explained before, meditation is a kind of presence, a watching of the flow of life. When there is meditation, impulses are fresh, spontaneous, "true," in contrast to those impulses which are automatic, preprogrammed by the mind for future use.

If I'm touching the right leg of someone and I find resonance, I know that the masculine part is able to meditate. In this very moment he is meditating with me, and the resonance tells me that it's not an accident but a developed capacity. Just from this contact I know already that the male part is able to be present and able to work in a successful way.

Now let's suppose that the left leg of the same person, the feminine part, doesn't have resonance. This means to me that her work will not be natural but forced, and that her impulses during work will come from "should" and "have to"... or perhaps that she doesn't work at all! Already we can see that there will be some trouble in the way these two parts relate to each other. The male is open, the female is closed, and they will not be able to communicate. The masculine part will suffer because he can feel the possibility for love is being lost, and the feminine won't know what to do about it. In this sense, resonance can tell you how relationship is going for the interior couple.

The problems of such an inner relationship will be reflected outside. The person I've just been describing, if he's a man, will fall in love with a woman who is closed, and he will struggle to relate with her, not understanding why things don't work. When

THE TWO SHORES OF LOVE

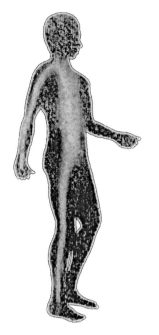

For the inner male: Job is okay. Meditation (presence) is okay. Relationship? He's ready, but she is not there!

this person comes to me, at the beginning of the session he will surely say that he has a problem in his relationship. But to me, the problem is not relationship. The problem is that the meditation of his own female side is not developed enough. Then his female side won't know what she wants to do in life, she won't be expressing herself. That which seemed at first to be a relationship question is actually a different one: how the female side can be reconnected with her own natural impulses and find a job she enjoys. During the session I will have to discover why her natural expression has been shut down.

I always consider these three aspects within a person—work, relationship, and meditation—as a unified circle, where each element is influencing the others.

Symptoms of difficulty in one area reveal a problem in the other two

I've discovered, working with the inner male and female of many people, that the problem the client presents to me is a symptom of dysfunction in the circle. And often this symptom comes to the surface in an area that is not the one where the problem really exists. This is natural. In the real area, where in fact the problem has its roots, the person doesn't want to change anything. In the real area, there will be an investment, something the subconscious doesn't want to disclose. Even the client doesn't know because it's hidden from his or her view.

I have learned to expect that the solution to the problem will be in one of the other two areas, and not in that area where the person experiences discomfort. So I am interested to hear about the symptoms only because they are a sure sign of where I will find nothing!

Bettina's session, which follows, is a sample of what I've been speaking about. Don't be concerned that you are unfamiliar with my method of revealing the two "inner" characters. I'll be explaining it fully in the next chapter. Also, there is a dialogue between myself (SP) and Bettina's two characters in this sample, a pattern which will be repeated in other sessions later on.

Zoo-keeping, perhaps

Bettina doesn't manage to find a man to be with. Especially in the last two months, she has been rejected by the men with whom she has had contact. Bettina is not unattractive, but at the moment she looks quite cold and unhappy.

I ask about her job. She does administrative work in a company that supports organic farmers. She likes the work itself, but the rapport among the team of people she has to work with is not good.

Bettina is a meditator but still, the resonance I find during the check is not very impressive. On the feminine side it is not immediately clear; I have to wait for some moments before her meditative quality reaches to me. On the male side there is none.

I place chairs for the two sides, and we start with the female. The female is the one doing the administrative job and she is solid, reliable, good at her work. When she speaks about her sadness that she can't find a man, she starts to cry.

I ask Bettina to move to the male's chair. In this new place, I ask her to become a man and to look at the woman who has been speaking from the other chair. Turning to him, I ask him, "How do you see her?" He answers that she's good at her job. She can do everything alone; she's completely self-sufficient. But he doesn't feel seen by her at all.

About himself he says that he doesn't find anything to do, he is without activity. Which means he doesn't work in the office. He feels longing in relation to her, and he too shows emotional distress that they cannot meet.

I ask Bettina to return to the first chair. Again she is to be the woman, now looking back at the man who just spoke. She reports that indeed, she cannot see him. He is in a fog. My sixth sense tells me that this could have something to do with the job.

SP (speaking to the female figure): If you can possibly imagine letting go of your business activity, you might be able to see him better.

This idea is such a shock for her that the contact between us is disrupted. So I ask Bettina to change chair again.

Bettina (male figure): Now she has gone away.
SP: Call her back.
Bettina (male, to the female): You have to come back!
SP: Is that an order, or an invitation?
Bettina (male, to the female): I would like you to be with me; I'm missing you.

Change over.

Bettina (female): Yes, now I can see him. He's not a very masculine man. It seems he's not doing anything. He's ineffective. Well, this is not the kind of person I wanted.

Change over—Bettina moves to the opposite chair.

SP (to the male): She doesn't accept you as you are, and this is making problems for you. You have two choices for solving your difficulty. The first solution is to find your own job: quit the administrative work and find an activity that has meaning for you. The second solution is to love yourself so much that her criticisms don't touch you. I think the second solution is more difficult, so why don't you try the first.

Bettina's male side starts looking into what that meaningful activity might be. It is for sure an outdoor job. Also, he loves animals—all kinds of animals. He would actually like to work in a zoo. "But," he concludes, "it's impossible." "Why not?" I say, "some people work in zoos. Why not you? At least you could inquire about what qualifications are needed."

We spend some more minutes dissolving his doubts that he is capable to find something he likes. I tell him to be open for an imperfect job in the beginning—anything where he can be outdoors. "It's always like that when you don't have experience. You have to start with something less than ideal, and then each change after that is an improvement."

I ask Bettina to change over again.

> *SP* (to the female): He wants to work in a zoo. What do you say to that?
> *Bettina* (female): It relaxes me. I like to see him active.
> *SP:* How is your relating to him in this moment?
> *Bettina* (female): Much better. He is stronger than before.
> *SP:* From your viewpoint, what sort of job do you think fits to him?
> *Bettina* (female): Something where he can move the body... (slowly considering) maybe handiwork.

Change over.

> *Bettina* (male): Handiwork? I couldn't do that—I'm a woman.
> *SP:* You're a man. Don't get too identified with which type of body you have.

Now that I feel he is convinced he can find his own work, we explore together the practicalities of learning something new, having enough money for that, and so on.

Bettina changes chairs again so that I can discuss with the female when she will quit her job. After some back-and-forth, she decides that she will stop in June, and right now it is the beginning of March.

She changes over for the last time.

Bettina (male): I feel nervous. No, it's not nervousness—it's excitement.

My main work in this session was to get the male to believe he could do something he'd never done before. He had never thought of changing jobs because the female's work was so easy for her. He had not realized that handing her the complete responsibility would leave him without definition, without strength, without a sense that he also has something to give.

Do you remember that Bettina brought to the session a relationship issue? As I said before, the resolution will be found in either of the other two areas: job, or meditation. In this case, the solution has come in the area of work.

Toward the beginning of the session when I said to the female, "Consider dropping the job and you will be able to see him better," it might have seemed to you like an illogical, intuitive leap. I can understand... and it's difficult to explain in words, but for me this "leap" is completely logical. Something is wrong with the job if the male is not participating in it, not expressing himself. And the shocked reaction of the female doesn't surprise me. It is simply a proof of how much she is attached to her occupation, and therefore of how much she doesn't recognize the male's dignity, or even his existence.

Bettina wanted to improve her connection to men without

touching the area of her job. But this is not possible! So you can see from this example why I say that you can't improve one area without changing something in the others.

Bettina went away completely happy. Her face was no longer full of clouds and discouragement—quite the opposite. She had never imagined that in only two hours she would be able to understand and change so many aspects of her situation.

CHAPTER 6

Setting up the Pair

As you have noticed already, there is a technique for separating and characterizing the two different polarities present inside you. In case you are curious to learn the procedure—either now or in the future—I'm including some instructions here that you can refer to any time. This "sculpturing" of the male and female figures is more easily understood by experiencing it directly rather than by reading about it. However, reading will at least give you a feeling for how the two personages can be brought into clear view.

I call this technique "setting up the pair." It requires a stage setting of two empty chairs in addition to the ones that the facilitator and the client already occupy. The empty chairs are placed facing each other with some distance in between, and these chairs will eventually represent the client's male and female aspects—the characters will each have their own designated space.

I should tell you now that this technique cannot be used all the time with just anybody and everybody. It depends very much on the client's ability to become one character, then the other—that is, it depends on the client's ability to be disidentified with both. Meditation is what prepares a person for this: by meditating one becomes acquainted with the feeling that "I am neither this nor that." Then both characters can be played in a light-hearted way.

To explain the process in detail, I will use a fictitious model as the client. Later on in this chapter you will have a real model so that you can apply the theory to a real-life situation.

How they feel, sitting with each other

Let's have our hypothetical client be a man. Once I have completed the energy check, I will be able to know which of his two sides I should choose to start setting up the pair. It will be the polarity that is more resonant and more full of love. It will probably be the part that the client is more familiar with, the one he uses more often in daily life. For this man, I now choose the female side.

I ask my client to sit on the chair representing his female, and we begin. He has his eyes closed while I recount to him the things I have seen about her in the energy reading of the left foot. I observe whether he is able to enter into this female character. The more he becomes the female and emanates her energy, the more I sense other things about her that come from my present moment of contact, not from the reading. After I finish what I have to say, I ask my client, "Can you feel the person I'm talking about?" If he says yes, I ask him to describe this woman, to choose some words appropriate to the experience which is arising. And so he, who has just become a "she," describes herself.

At this point I ask the client to change chairs and go to the opposite one, leaving his inner woman (figuratively speaking) still seated in the chair where he has just been. Now he sits facing the inner woman—who is, of course, not visible to the physical eye but rather to the inner eyes. I say to my client, "Be a man. As a man, look back at the woman. You can do it with your eyes open or closed, whichever is easier for you. I would like you to describe

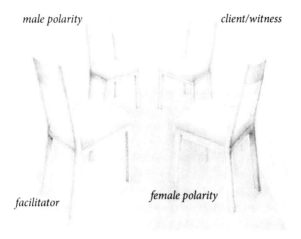

male polarity *client/witness*

facilitator *female polarity*

her from your own point of view, and it's okay if your description is different than my description of her, or even her own."

And he starts. The way he perceives her may be surprising. For example, what she referred to as vulnerability and softness he may perceive as weakness. That which she has defined as calmness he may call inactivity. The qualities that she considered peaceful he thinks are simply boring.

It can happen that the second figure, in this case the male, starts to talk about his own feelings instead of describing her, the first figure. Then I interrupt him and invite him to continue his description of the female—the moment to talk about himself will come later. For now, he should tell me how he sees her because it may be the only moment in the session when I can hear about that.

And so the masculine part resumes his description, focusing only on her. When he's finished, I ask him simply to feel himself seated across from a person who *is* as he described, and to tell me his immediate experience. My exact question is, "What kind of person do you become in her presence?" Common responses are

"I feel bigger than her" or "I feel smaller." Other times the inner man may answer "I feel angry," "I want to go away." Or even perhaps, "I'm full of admiration for her," "I want to be like her," or "I'm jealous."

After this self-description from the male part, I invite the client to change chairs, and return to the place that represents the feminine. Now I ask the female to tell her view of the man who sits across from her. Again, I may have to remind her to stay with the description of him first and to tell me her own feelings or reactions afterward.

When this entire process is finished, I invite the client to leave the two chairs and to return to the one in which he started the session, facing me. From this position, my client can better observe the "couple" with whom I have been interacting. I call this third chair the place of the witness. From here, there is nothing to do— only to observe, only to watch.

Often at this point the client needs a break. I can understand, because it is really work—feeling oneself and observing the other. From the witnessing chair, the client can take note of all the tensions and conflicts that have just been expressed from the other two chairs but he can do nothing about them. It's good to just rest for a moment, and take distance.

In fact, this distance is quite important. It is the essence of a Star Sapphire session.

Indications of resonance in the characters

In order for the inner relationship to improve, my client needs to have a place within himself where he is content with the situation exactly as it is now. This doesn't mean that the inner man and inner woman have to be happy, it simply means that the client has to find within himself a contentment not based on the satisfaction of desires: a contentment which is, in fact, a meditative state. This is the reason I ask the client to sit on the chair of the witness—to have him return to an understanding that this moment is fine, just as it is.

From this place of observation, he manages to have a wider perspective of the relation between his female and male. Their relating started long, long ago, its future is still unknown, and this moment in the middle of the continuum is okay as it is. Everything is proceeding as it should, and one can have trust in the ongoing evolution.

From my check at the beginning of the session, I should already know if my client has a capacity for the state of meditation. A significant resonance in any chakra will be the proof. As far as witnessing is concerned, the two legs don't need to have resonance.

However, when the set-up is complete and we start to open up a new dimension of contact between the male and female, things will go more easily if the client has some resonance in one or both legs. I have already observed these legs during the resonance check. So while I set up the pair, I also watch the two characters closely at that time to see if there is some indication of the resonance that I expect to be there.

Resonance in a character, as it speaks from its own chair, will affect me in the same way as I said before—my interior space feels enriched and expanded. But also there are other affirmative signs in the behavior of the character. A flowing river of impulses from within makes the character independent, self-directed. He or she will no longer be able to take orders from anyone who assumes superiority. The character knows very precisely which activities bring joy, and willingly takes responsibility, meaning that he or she is able to initiate a response to an outer situation. When I see these things, it confirms the reading of resonance.

On the other hand if I see that the person—the character— likes to do what somebody else proposes, is not self-directed, is not independent, is not responsible for their own joy, it confirms a reading of no-resonance. I never think of no-resonance as a bad thing, but simply as an engagement in desire. This sort of person is waiting to get things from outside, to be nourished and guided. They are simply not yet aware that everything they need is inside.

No-resonance should always be seen as an absence of self rather than as a negativity. If you see it as a negativity, you start judging. If you see it as an absence of self, you will perceive it as a perfectly good starting place for finding the self. In fact, at one point in our history we all started there!

The importance of relaxed witnessing

The things I'm going to say next are quite technical, more suited to people who will formally study the method of Star Sapphire. But regardless, please read this section once or at least look at the circular diagrams, to note that there are different conditions a therapist has to work with. Of course if you're really not interested in the specifics of how to help a client, you can go directly to the box with the next example.

To continue with the subject of resonance... When I watch the characters I see one of these resonance patterns, which I have numbered from 0 to 5—the reason will be clear. The circles are

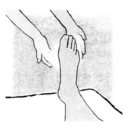 representing resonance in the male and the female figures during the set-up of the pair. Normally it corresponds to the resonance in the bottom of the feet, observed during the resonance check, so as you look at these grey and white circles you can imagine you are touching the left and right foot. Dark grey is for the absence of resonance and white is for its presence.

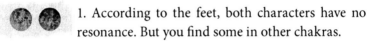 0. In this pattern, both characters have no resonance. You see them having expectations of each other. There is also no resonance in any of the chakras.

Supportive response: You should not set up the pair. Try to catch this situation ahead of time and then use a different approach—for example, teaching the client how to meditate.

1. According to the feet, both characters have no resonance. But you find some in other chakras.

Supportive response: Try to feel intuitively which character is closer to its own loving impulses, closer to its creativity, and help this one to feel trust. Help this one to find some simple choice of its own—even if only the body position it wants to have right now.

2. One character can find its centeredness when alone, but when you put it together with the non-resonant polarity, this centeredness is lost due to some misunderstanding about love.

Supportive response: Encourage the more loving, centered character to follow its impulses and to live life accordingly.

3. Clearly, one character already lives the way it wants. The other one is collapsed and not functioning yet.

Supportive response: Work with the second figure, the darker one. Try to help it organize priorities, and take steps to have the life go in a way it prefers.

4. The first character has presence continuously. The second character has presence when it is alone. But when it is with the first, centeredness is lost due to some misunderstanding about love.

Supportive response: Clear up the misunderstanding. A new

kind of "togetherness" is growing in which each party has complete independence.

 5. Both characters have presence, and neither of them loses it when they are together.

Supportive response: There is no need to adjust the balance between male and female, but rather to resolve a specific problem in one polarity. And so, you work with that one only.

Most people, naturally, fall into categories 1 and 2 when they are just beginning to know their inner polarities. Therefore, most sessions only invite a change in the first, or stronger polarity. When I say "a change" I don't mean something for the character to do, but rather something to stop doing! The first polarity has to relax more, to become a watcher, or a witness, of what happens by itself. And then I try to convey to him or her a single, simple message: that when you follow your relaxed, natural impulse, the other will always be benefited.

If the first polarity is able to relax and trust in itself even when the second polarity complains or protests, it will start to have an indirect influence on the second polarity. The passion, the certainty, the joy with which the first polarity does things will spread as a nourishing atmosphere to the second one and, over time, the second one will relax also. But it takes a while. Normally I see my clients only once in six months, because then I can observe if the relaxation of the more open polarity is invisibly spreading to the polarity more closed, and a new balance has been achieved without effort.

I say all these things to communicate to you the importance of relaxed witnessing in resolving every difficulty between the polarities. According to my experience, growth cannot happen in any other way.

The polarities go "on stage"

Now I will show you a real set-up, as I promised, with a client who is not just hypothetical!

A special gift for design

Leonard is an engineer living in Düsseldorf, Germany. He has worked for Volvo in the past; now he is self-employed, designing car engines for Daimler-Benz and machine tools for Tetra Pak using special three-dimensional computers. Even though his job is well-paid, he is always short of cash because his expenses are high. He told me that he rents an office for 1,200 euros per month. He wanted to stop leasing that office, but somehow he postponed canceling the contract; when he finally got around to it he was two weeks too late, and according to the rules he will have to continue leasing it one year longer.

He is taking the session from me today because he is not feeling good within himself on the subject of work. He says it is not flowing, sometimes there are no jobs. Anyway he would like to stop and take a break, but he cannot because of the expenses.

The resonance check tells me that it is true: he has a problem about work. The second chakra is quite imploded, or inwardly collapsed, and not resonant. However, Leonard has an abundance of resonance in the heart and at the top of the head, also a significant resonance in the throat. The right leg is intermittently resonant, like a blinking light. The left leg is not resonant, and there is an image of someone who I would call "bürgerlich"—she is somewhat round, maybe even fat in the bum, and sitting with smug satisfaction next to the kitchen table of her own house. The important thing is that she has managed to be secure. There is a look of determination on her face, and the sense of having succeeded in "holding it all together."

We start with setting up the pair. I choose Leonard's male side as the figure with more potential. I show him which chair is the inner man's place and I ask him to sit there.

SP: I'm going to describe the person that I saw in your right foot. I want you to tune into this person, and then describe him yourself from inside.

Leonard: Yes.

SP: Close your eyes. (long pause) I see this person having quite a brilliant technical mind, but it feels like this mind is only a small part of him. Actually he has other parts that like to walk in the sun, that like to meet people. I feel these other parts wide… they are more connected to the unknown, and to adventure. But, this person has one unfortunate habit: that when you give him a technical problem to solve, he automatically does it. He has been doing it for so long… It's like a dog—when you give him a bone, he chews. Technical problems are like bones that you chew on, trying to find the answer. So, I feel this man has a very good mind but he is longing not to use it all the time. Can you feel the person I'm speaking about?

Leonard: Yes.

SP: Can you choose some words of your own to describe him?

Leonard (male): Yeah, when I get a problem, I don't give up until it's solved! It keeps my mind very busy. I feel I have to find the solution, then I can relax and feel satisfied with myself. I see that there are other parts—I like to be in nature, to be in the mountains, to walk without a goal, to see far away in the distance. I try to give myself space for these things, but it is not always easy because I'm so occupied with work.

SP: Okay. That's enough, unless there's something else you want to say.

Leonard (male): No.

SP: Open your eyes, then, and change over to the other side.

Leonard moves to the opposite chair.

SP: I would like you to be female, and as a female to look back at the man who just spoke. You can do this with your eyes open or closed, whichever is easier. I'd like to hear a description of how you see him, and it may be different than his description of himself, or my description of him.

Leonard (female): I like him. He's a good man. Sometimes he is much better than me. I am smaller, and I don't know so much. I'm more simple...

SP: Can you keep on describing him, even if it is to say, "He's bigger than me," but keep the focus on the other side, for now.

Leonard (female): He can concentrate very well. Yes, he's very good.

SP: Do you see him concentrating right now?

Leonard (female): He's relaxed right now. He's enjoying—well, he is trying to enjoy. It looks like he would like to have more time for enjoying.

SP: Good, that's enough. When you sit with a person like that, what do you become? Now you can speak about yourself. You said you feel a bit inferior to him?

Leonard (female): Ja... well, he talks very easily with other people and I can't... I'm a bit shy and I try to hide myself. I feel more insecure than he does. I'm dependent on him. In one way, I like it; but in another way, I don't like it.

SP: Change over.

Leonard moves to the opposite chair.

SP (to the male): As a man, look back at the woman, and tell me how you see her. What kind of person sits in the other chair?

Leonard (male): She's... I wouldn't say lazy, but... she doesn't take much care of herself. She's simple, and simplicity could be a nice thing but this is different—like when you don't care for your body, you don't brush your teeth, don't take a shower—as though it doesn't matter. She likes simple things. She likes to "get the order" (sic), she doesn't like to think on her own.

SP: I didn't understand; can you say it again?

Leonard (male): Ja... it's more easy for her if somebody tells her, "Please clean the floor here," and then she does it; but she doesn't know how to decide on her own.

SP: Uh-huh. What happens in you when you sit with a person like that?

Leonard (male): I get impatient. For me it's so natural to be independent. I don't like when somebody gives me an order. I like to figure it out on my own, and I have the capacity to do that. And when the things to do become too simple, I get bored.

SP: Are you bored now? Or are you saying that if you lived the way she lives, you would be bored?

Leonard (male): In this moment of my life, I'm bored. I would like to have more responsibility. And I like having connections with people. Not to give them orders, but to be responsible—to have connection and be part of a team.

SP: What do you think is preventing you from doing the things that you want to do? I notice that when you sit with her, you start to remember things that you'd actually like to do in your life, which you're not yet doing.

Leonard (male): Yes, that's right.

SP: Is she preventing you in some way?

Leonard (male): I don't think she does it on purpose, but anyway I have to keep myself back. If I don't keep myself back, she doesn't understand and she feels inferior and… she can get sad. I don't like that.

SP: It sounds like she can manipulate you just by being sad. All she has to do is feel inferior and sad, and then you stop doing what you like.

Leonard (male): I don't think she does it on purpose, I think it's more an unconscious habit. If you don't have the ability to decide on your own… I adjust to her habit, because I don't want to blame somebody by saying, "You must understand this, it's not so complicated." Then I keep myself back.

SP: Okay, I understand you. Now you can sit here in the third chair, the witnessing chair.

This time I am going to keep you hanging about the ending! Leonard is going to be a serial—we will hear his story in several parts, interspersed in various chapters of this book. But for now, you can start being the detective and ask yourself some questions.

Do you agree with me that the male side was the right one to start with? In which way is it evident that he has the more potential of the two?

Which pattern do you think we are dealing with? Is it number one, where both male and female are not resonant, and the only resonance that supports my work with this pair comes from some other part of the body?

Is it pattern number two, where one of the partners has resonance, but is not able to live his truth because of thinking he needs to adjust to the other?

Or is it number three, where one part has resonance, but the weaker side is not yet living according to its internal directives?

If it is number one or number two, I will work only with one side. And if my guess about starting with the right side is correct, then we would work only with the right side in this session—supporting the masculine part to go forward with his things. The female is allowed to stay exactly as she is.

If the pattern is number three, we will work with the left side in this session.

So what do you think? It's a mystery! Every session is a mystery. And I won't tell you just yet in which chapter you can find the solution.

CHAPTER 7

What is Love

Probably I'll surprise you. The title of the chapter could have led you to imagine some beautiful and romantic things about love, but instead I'm going to talk about problems. These are problems that occur between the inner man and inner woman—in this chapter the superficial ones, and in the next chapter some deeper problems connected to their essence. I am hoping to give you insight into a few points that may have escaped your attention before. Then, perhaps in less time than you think, you may start to experience a quality of love that leaves you wide and unbounded both inside and outside. But first one has to face the encumbrances.

In the sections that follow you will read about four kinds of difficulties which I call "relational" and which concern indiscriminately the male and female. I mean to say that the cause of disharmony can be traced to a wrong style of relating or to a socially imposed idea, or even to a superficial cause not connected to the essence of the two characters. Once you have figured out which is the wrong idea causing a character to act in a certain way, it's usually enough just to see it and then the dynamic between your male and female can change dramatically.

The need for independence

The relations in which we are engaged inside and outside mirror each other, but with one important difference. When we move toward the outer world, there seem to be many options. If we don't get what we want from one person, we can go to somebody else. But in our inner world, in the subconscious, it is not like that. One polarity wants to receive love from the other as if it represents the only existing source. When this source is closed or dry, the first polarity doesn't perceive any other possibility for exchange. And that is why, even if outside you go in search of a new partner in order to feel satisfied, inside you feel frustrated because you are searching for a love that never arrives. If you want to put an end to suffering, you first have to break this unconscious inner dependency.

In the interior relationship, there can be one polarity that doesn't respect the other's need for independence. One polarity doesn't give the other the space to be alone. Sometimes it's the male that doesn't allow any time-out to the other, sometimes it's the female.

However, the need for aloneness is a real need; no one can survive without it. It all depends on how you live this independence. There are two ways—one succeeds, while the other fails. The way that works is what I call "love." It's a yes to oneself, a relaxing into one's energy, letting choices come from a flowing source inside. The way that doesn't work is a reaction to the other, a "no." You close up, you construct a wall around yourself, you become unreachable. Actually, in this second mode one doesn't obtain freedom at all but its opposite: one remains tied to the other by a desire, even if it's negative. For example, if it is the man who wants independence and he chooses reaction, saying "no" to the woman, the result is that she will try to possess him more and more. And he, more and more, will want to get away. That's why I say that they are bound together by desire.

When an interior couple has this problem I have to know, as a therapist, which of the two parts is actually the more capable to be on its own, alone but in a "yes" to life. It's not always the one demanding freedom! Sometimes I have to say to the possessive polarity, "You don't need to control the other, you can create your happiness yourself." But other times I feel that with just a tiny "click," the reactive one could become creative, and then I say to that one, "You have no need to react, you can relax in your love."

Judgments

Now, just to be fair to the two sexes, I'm going to reverse the example. This time, imagine that it's the inner man who prevents the inner woman from having any independence. But he is tricky. First, he establishes his superiority by saying, "I see things more clearly than you do," or "My point of view is more trustworthy." After he has put himself on the pedestal, his judgments begin: "You are not strong enough," "You are too passive," "You're too emotional," "You take too much time," "You can't earn money by being so sensitive," "You don't know the world." The woman will be confused. The man is negating all of her best qualities. So by this trick of making judgments, one polarity can literally take the wind out of the other's sails.

In this case, the woman will have to learn to trust in her qualities, to give them value. Life would not be much fun if there were only toughness and no softness, only reason without intuition, only hard-earned cash and no sentiment. The woman has to watch out, because if she starts to believe the male's point of view she will shrink.

Economic roots

Another cause of disharmony between the inner man and woman is related to economics. In the ideal situation, they both take care. The male part follows his natural inclinations, and money arrives. Same for the female. It can happen that money arrives through the skills of one part, and the other part is regenerating energy—this is also a case in which both parts are completely responsible for the economy.

Unfortunately, it's an ideal that is almost never reached. In most cases, one part of the body carries the weight of financial responsibility for both. This situation, which is not natural, causes a disequilibrium in the system. There are social reasons, of course. One is the old idea that the man should provide financially by going to the office, while the woman should stay at home. Men have gathered power by this social convention and have preferred to leave women in a position of weakness, uneducated and incapable of work.

It happens often in sessions that I see interior couples in which the man tries to convince the woman that it is not necessary for her to work. It's a way to confuse her, to give her the idea that she will never be able to take care of herself on a financial level. This way, the man constructs for himself an illusion of happiness—the woman is dependent on him, she will never be able to leave him, and in this sense his future is secure.

More rarely, it is the inner woman who is earning for both. By chance, I see this kind of session often because I am quite the same type, and naturally I attract people similar to myself.

The quality of the female side is less connected to business and more linked to art, beauty, and sensitivity, but this, too, can be carried to an extreme. If she is in the habit of earning money by means of her capacities, she will be protective of these. For example, if she sells jewelry in a very elegant shop where the atmosphere is silent, she won't permit the inner man to be vital, to play around, to make jokes and gross movements. Because of her error in perspective, she may actually consider the male inferior and prevent him from contacting his own qualities. Then slowly slowly, over time, he is reduced into being her servant.

These examples were extreme. Let me give you one that is more common.

It is normally the male side of a person that takes responsibility for the job, as he is the more outgoing character. Being so occupied with the duty of earning money, he hasn't any time to discover his deeper resources and so he remains disconnected inside. That's why his decision about which work to do is superficial, based on other people's ideas of suitable and lucrative professions. When such a person comes to me (who can be either a woman or a man), the male side is not aware that he doesn't like his job. On the contrary, he will tell me that the job is going well. But when I look more closely into the right leg, I see that this job is "deadening" him, not giving any vitality to the body. Now, the female part of the same person may have a sensitivity and a capacity to love that is very developed, but she has never carried these abilities into any concrete form of work so she doesn't realize their value. The male part, naturally, has never helped her in this because he's convinced that she is not able to earn money with her qualities.

This female part will surely tell me that she has to follow the directives of the male. She thinks there is no other choice for her in life. But she doesn't see that it is simply a question of economics: the minute she supports herself economically, she will no longer have to take direction from him.

If, as a therapist, I can help her to feel her strength and to take responsibility for her physical survival using her own qualities, this will also have an effect on the male part. In the beginning he will resist because he doesn't want to lose the security that her obedience gives to him. But after a while he starts to notice how exhausted he is. Then I encourage him to take a "vacation," a period of rest. This is a real shock for someone who has always believed he has to fight to survive. He cannot imagine work chosen for the satisfaction it brings, because he has not yet found the source of such work within himself. He will need a few months' break and some relaxation before this connection to his interior can happen, so a "vacation" is the best thing!

And I remind the male of one more aspect to be considered: his behavior up to now has prevented the female from standing on her own legs. When she starts to do that, their relationship will improve!

Generally, my sessions have success when I can help the loving side to take economic responsibility and the disconnected side to be more playful and less serious about money.

The expectations of marriage

I'm about to speak on a delicate subject: marriage. I don't mean any external marriage involving another person but only the one on the inside of which you may not be aware.

I want to clarify immediately that I don't have anything against marriage in itself—personally I have had good experience. But there are many ideas linked to the institution of marriage which can suffocate the relation between a man and a woman. These are ideas which prevent a person from growing in love, from becoming an individual. These ideas should be looked at again, because they are a big cause of dependency between the interior polarities.

Sometimes, when I watch a dialogue between the inner man and inner woman, one of the two (maybe the male) says, "I have to do whatever she wants." Or the contrary (maybe the female),

"He needs me, I am not free to come and go." These are cases in which I feel the presence of a marriage. I mean a certain type of bonding, like the two vacuum cleaners I talked about in the third chapter having decided to be vacuum cleaners happily ever after. The difference between relationship and marriage is the mental decision to make this tie permanent. If the choice to be married comes from the inner woman, she decides that in order not to be alone she will obligate herself to satisfy the expectations of the inner man, who also doesn't want to stay alone.

It can happen that I say to this inner woman, "I think you should get a divorce." This divorce has nothing to do with anyone on the outside, but rather with the inner male of the same person, and my intention in proposing this is to get the inner woman more familiar with aloneness. Certainly I don't follow this direction unless I feel she has developed an appropriate inner strength—otherwise she could fall into desperation.

If the feminine in question is ready and willing to make this experiment, I say, "And now that you are divorced, how do you feel?" She responds in many ways, which I summarize: "It's like I have a house all my own. Now I am surrounded by a space that belongs to me. My choices come from inside me, no one directs me from outside. I seem to breathe better." When I ask her whether she wants to meet with the man she will say, "I have no precise plans; probably I would like to see him now and then."

What happens to the inner man in this case? If he is able to speak about his real feelings, rather than having reactions or trying to control her, he is going to say, "I feel as if I've lost something. I have fear to stay alone. I don't know what I want to do now." I leave him in this situation for a bit, and return to the woman. I ask her to follow her impulses in some simple task, like choosing a place to stand in the room, or like finding a rhythm as she moves her weight from one leg to the other. When I go back again to the man and ask him how he feels about her choice, he says, "She seems to be happy. I'd like to be able to be happy like that." Or else, "Seeing her happy gives me the freedom to think about what I want to do to be happy myself."

Michael had an "inner marriage," and to rearrange his marital bliss took a very, very short time—not more than fifteen minutes!

A successful divorce

Michael works in a wellness center, where he is part-time receptionist, part-time bartender. He is attending a seminar I am presenting to the center's staff, about how to feel fulfilled in your working life, and he reports that his levels of satisfaction are mediocre. He actually likes both of his jobs but when he looks more carefully at each moment, he feels that he is doing things mechanically, just to get the job done, and receiving no joy from his movements.

This time I do the resonance check surrounded by the group members, who are his friends.

The check shows that the jobs are right—his second chakra is in good order, also the heart and the upper chakras are fine. The problem is in the legs. Both are dark and not resonant. The female is in a "no." The male side shows a gesture of consoling her, trying to make her feel better, and he's saying, "There, there, it's not so bad as all that."

Fortunately, Michael is quite honest when we set up his pair. The female can feel her closure. She crosses her arms over her chest in an attempt to keep the man at a distance. The male side feels sad, angry, and frustrated that he cannot connect with her. When Michael goes back to the witnessing chair, he visibly relaxes. He says, "The other two places are very uncomfortable! I want to sit here and just let them do their thing."

Michael's male side is a rather fatherly type; he reminds me of a married man, rather than a single man. So I simply ask Michael to sit on the male chair and I question the male side, referring to the empty chair in front of him, "Are you married to her?" He answers, "Yes." And I ask him if he could consider the possibility to get divorced. He is quite surprised by the request, but he agrees to try it.

> SP (to the male): And I would like you to move out of the house you share with your wife, and get your own space. This doesn't mean that there is no love, only that each of you has a space or a territory that is your own. Can you actually move your chair now to another location in the room that represents a house or an apartment that is your own?

Michael moves the chair of the male part one meter to the right, and now he is sitting partially behind me, protected a little from any direct contact with the woman.

> *Michael* (male): I feel a little afraid. Who will I be without her?

Change over.

> SP (to the female): He is getting a divorce. What happens in you?
> *Michael* (female): I also feel fear. I need him so that I can know who I am.
> SP: Close your eyes. And now imagine that you are living in your own house, which is going to be represented by your own body. Breathe in such a way that you expand into every corner of your house, so that it is filled by you… Breathe into the belly and into the legs… Let the energy flow into your arms…

The female has already started to breathe. And suddenly, before I can say anything more, she starts to laugh, and then to cry—then to laugh and cry both at once! Her energy is surging up from inside and spilling over, like water from an overfull cup. She starts to breathe even deeper, and her joy is growing and growing. She is shaking her head, as if she can't believe it, and all the while she can't stop smiling.

SP: You see, being married to him, you got a totally wrong identity. That was not you at all. This is you! This laughter, this lightness, this overflowing love. Keep breathing it.

Change over.

SP (to the male): She is doing quite well. How are you?
Michael (male): This is a very new condition... it's okay, I will get used to it.

I didn't tell you that Michael is a meditator. The explosive energy of the being that emerged from his feminine side is a result of following the path of meditation, an unexpected flowering that occurred in the very moment of our session. Reading about it, the point might not seem obvious because what happened to Michael's feminine side is a kind of quantum leap, something which is not explainable rationally. You have to just live it in first-person. It's an experience of pure love.

In the case of Michael, the end of the session showed a masculine side quite able to accept the new situation. It doesn't always happen like that. There are other times when breaking the tie of dependency appears to be a destructive process because only one part manages to find a new mode of behavior while the other one feels lost and uncomfortable. But if the first polarity has enough trust in itself and continues to act as a person "unmarried," she will help the second one also to experiment with his own possibilities for independence and self-sufficiency. Then the two parts will be able to meet each other in a more satisfying way than before.

When the two polarities are each in a state of relaxation, they are naturally attracted to each other like positive and negative poles of electricity. Since they can't really get away from each other

THE TWO SHORES OF LOVE

the right question to ask is, in which style do they want to relate? As two beggars, or as two mature individuals?

Read this example to have an idea.

Daring to... take a walk

Marco is working as a male nurse in a hospital on the outskirts of Milan. He just got his driving license so now he can travel to work by car—he lives nearby in the countryside.

Telling me his history, he says he used to have an exploratory life style, many women, many experiences... up until two years ago. At that time he had a relationship with a married woman, which was painful. Then a second girlfriend came into his life. The situation was alive but difficult. The new girlfriend was waiting for him to drop the unavailable one. Eventually he did, and he decided to go in the "opposite direction." He had always been against marriage but now he decided to experience that, too. So he married the new girlfriend and they are expecting a baby in one more month.

He says that he used to have blissful, magical moments and now he feels dull, flat, and bored. His question is, "Am I on my track?"

The resonance check shows that Marco's female side has no resonance. At first I see only black. And then, enveloped in the darkness, I see a Madonna figure, head bent gently over a child in her arms. It's like a still-life portrait.

In the masculine side there is a steady resonance, not the maximum but enough to make it constant. The male part has the spirit of adventure: he's inquisitive, ready to explore.

This is how I respond to Marco's question: "Yes, in one sense you are on your track—and everybody is. Everybody is bringing dark parts of themselves into the outer mirror and then engaging themselves with the projection. So in this sense, you cannot go on a wrong track. The question is, can you deal with this engagement in a new way?

"Your feminine side is in a darkness. And right now it is taking you into darkness and you go without complaint."

Then I start the experiential part of the session with the male side, asking Marco to close his eyes while I find words to express what I encountered in his right leg.

> *SP:* This is the person who just got his driver's license. He's an explorer, and you need a car to get to the new places. I feel this person has a strong sense of smell. As if he's arriving in a new environment and checking the scent in the air. And he's even able to make subtle distinctions in smell. To him one corner of an Arabian market smells different than another.
>
> *Marco* (male): This man does not want to take instructions from anyone.

Marco changes the place.

> *SP* (to the female): How do you see him?
> *Marco* (female): Sooner or later he's going to go away from me.
> *SP:* Who are you?
> *Marco* (female): My body is made of earth. His is of fire. We don't connect. We cannot come together.

I'm not surprised when she says they don't connect—in this she tells the truth.

Marco then moves to the male's chair. I ask him if there is something he can do to nourish himself. He answers that when he was a child, he used to walk in the woods with his grandmother early in the morning. He enjoyed it immensely but his parents decided that it was not safe, and they prevented him from continuing.

> *SP:* You think you would like to walk in the woods? How often?
> *Marco* (male): Every day.
> *SP:* Which hour can you do that?
> *Marco* (male): Six o'clock in the morning

Change to the female side.

SP (to the female): He's going to leave the house for a walk in the woods each morning at 6:00. Any response?

Marco (female, to the male): You shouldn't go. It's not safe. Anyway, I don't think our neighbors will approve.

Change to the male side.

Marco (male): You're probably right. Okay, I won't go.

SP: The woman has only to say a few words expressing her interest in safety and social image, and you are dissuaded?

Marco (male): I feel that if I go into the woods I'm betraying her.

SP: It's the opposite! This is the only loving thing to do! This is the best possible choice, for her and for you. Following your truth creates love inside yourself. And this love will then pour over to her.

Marco (male): (silence)

SP: Are you going to go?

Marco (male): Yes.

Change over to the female.

Marco (female): I don't like it. I don't want him to leave. I need him. (Silence) Also, I feel envy. He can move around so easily. He has fun and I don't have any joy. I feel dead when he's not around.

Change over to the male.

SP (to the male): Are you going to go? She's using all the tricks to prevent you: security, image, need, envy...

Marco (male): Yes, I will have to trust that if I love myself it will be good for her.

Change over.

SP (to the female): What could you do to be creative when he's not there?

Marco (female): Be with the child. (frowning) But he too will go away in a few years. He will go out to play, and I will be alone again... Another dream broken.

SP: So imagine the child is grown up some years and he also is away. What would you enjoy to do with your free time? (pause) Dancing?… flowers?… meditation?

The feminine of Marco is not touched until I say the word 'meditation'. Suddenly she wakes up.

SP: At the beginning of this session, you said that you were earth and he was fire, and you could not connect. When you are in meditation and he is out in nature, do you feel connected? *Marco* (female): (first looking surprised, and then smiling) Yes!

Love can happen only when you trust in yourself. To be loving is your very nature! And the best way to let love flow is just to make sure you are content with the things you are doing, now… and in every "now."

CHAPTER 8

More Intractable Difficulties in Meeting Each Other

Previously I exposed some "relational" misunderstandings between the masculine and feminine, and now I am going to focus on deeper impediments to love. They are deeper because they involve the very nature of the two polarities. In some cases, each of the polarities is carrying its essential characteristic to an extreme. In other cases one polarity's inherent difficulty is causing a problem between the two; then the second, with all good intentions, cannot resolve it. Finally, I will speak about the toughest cases I encounter: where one character is so much admired or elevated that the other one, by trying to emulate the first, loses its own nature. You will see what havoc this creates!

We start with an example in which the two natures go to their extremes and the two characters don't manage to absorb the reciprocal energies—and so they cannot meet, at least not right now. This example comes from a long training course in Sweden where the theme was work, and I was the third of many leaders to offer direction. With me, the people had just finished an exercise where they were getting to know the masculine and feminine aspects of themselves. When I asked if anyone felt disturbed by a lack of harmony between them, one woman requested my help.

She was about forty years old and her name was Helga. Helga had an imposingly sturdy body and she dressed like a man, in T-shirt and loose pants. But I discovered, to my surprise, that she was doing work that I considered feminine: she co-ordinated advanced instruction for nurses in a Swedish hospital. In addition to that, she traveled for two weeks each month to Moldavia, in the former Soviet Union, to do the same thing as part of a development program sponsored by the Swedish government. In the town where she went in Moldavia there was no heating in the houses nor in the working places, nor was there any hot water for a shower. Helga had learned to wash herself in very cold water!

The first sentence she said to me was, "During this training course I have decided to live." Which meant to me that before the course started, she didn't want to live. "Were you suicidal?" I asked. "I've never thought about suicide directly," she said, "but I've always done things that put my life in danger."

With Helga, I was limited to an energy reading because it was the tail-end of a group session and I had only a few remaining moments. During the check, I saw in her left leg the image of a nymph in a forest, sensitive, almost transparent. She stood beside a tree, but she could easily have slipped behind it and disappeared from one moment to the next. This person for sure was not the one choosing dangerous activities, but also it was true that if the body were to die she wouldn't mind too much.

The masculine side of Helga was the opposite. The inner man had a physical body that was quite strong, also a bit awkward. He looked for some engagement, some battle where he could prove his own strength to himself.

Speaking briefly to the feminine, I discovered that she felt responsible for the work as a nurse but she didn't like it. The man, on the other hand, was enthusiastic about his work. When I asked him if he liked to do it in Sweden and in Moldavia, his answer was "only in Moldavia." I had suspected as much, because Moldavia was the ideal place to put himself to the test, to prove his strength and his ability to resist under difficult circumstances. I said to Helga, in conclusion, that to me it seemed important that neither part of her liked the work in Sweden.

Although I didn't tell her this, my guess is that these two persons, the nymph and the macho man, will not be able to meet each other—at least not now. They are each going toward their farthest extreme. The transparent nymph is about to disappear into nothingness. He, on the other hand, is busy becoming more substantial by demonstrating his strength in a place where it is difficult to survive. Deep down these two energies would like to meet, but they don't know how to do it. And so they make compromises. In this case, the feminine of Helga has adjusted herself to the male's need for challenge, when actually a nymph would freeze in Moldavia!

Helga needs to meditate over a longer period of time; after that, the female will have a more positive evaluation of herself and she will choose a life style closer to what she really wants.

Please allow me a digression at this point. Helga's story has reminded me to mention a typical characteristic of male energy that can have inadvertent consequences. A masculine energy like Helga's that is pushing to become bigger and stronger, if it is not tempered by any contact with the feminine, will tend to keep going and going, stretching its boundaries until it encounters a limitation, a barrier—until it gets stopped. This is the cause of war: two masculine energies seeking to expand crash into each other. And in the collision the energy which could have been constructive turns destructive, with death as an outcome. So it is no small matter for the planet that we don't let the feminine in ourselves disappear—the tendency for which you can see in this sample.

One polarity with low self-esteem

We change the scene completely and enter into a relationship in which the masculine and feminine, coming to know something more about themselves, are able to meet in a better way.

Silent lake with no ripples

This session is about Charlotte, a German woman who is quite young—just twenty-four years old—but mature for her age. She tells me that she has never found a man who would stay with her, they literally escape. And, ironically, she has a weakness for athletes, particularly those who run!

During the resonance check I am able to see the characters in Charlotte's legs very distinctly. In the right leg there is a man who runs away from me and gives the sensation of not wanting to be seen. He takes refuge in a small forest, running until he is sure to find himself alone, at which point he relaxes. He is in a clearing in the forest, a place covered in grass, which is known only to him.

This is the type of person who complicates his life by trying to do his own thing inside a wall that keeps others out.

In Charlotte's left leg I see a young woman in a rose garden. I see her sitting with her eyes closed, meditating, but her energy quality is sad and too much alone. I am particularly struck by two things. First, she has tried everything she can think of to make a connection with the man, and the efforts have come to a standstill; every road is blocked. And second, I see a picture of a placid lake, waveless. This is a symbol for me of the feminine energy without any male influence "making waves." She doesn't like the flatness of it—when that feeling comes she wants to leave the body and fly into the spirit realms like a bird. This "leaving" is not healthy.

I start setting up the pair from the masculine side. He has his eyes closed while I tell him about my pictures, and then he reports that he experiences himself near his secret place but up in a tree! I ask him if he can see the feminine. "Far away. For me she is flat, boring." He says of himself that he loves adventure.

When the feminine looks at the masculine, she says that he is a person she can't reach. The pain of it begins to show on her face; she is holding back tears, as if she decided long ago that crying is not going to help.

I ask her to look at me and to tell me, "I love him,"—referring to the man. She discovers, in doing it, that she does feel love and that it's not important whether the male responds, at least to this expression of it.

I ask her to say directly to the man, "I love you," and then immediately turn to look at me again. This is to help her practice staying in the state of love without expectations; if she continues to look at the man after having said "I love you," she may fall back into expecting love in return. We do this little exercise together a few times.

Charlotte goes back to the cushion representing the male side. I ask to the man if he has been touched by what is happening. He says, "I have come down from my tree; now I'm on the ground. She's not so boring any more. It would be possible for me to move closer to her, but I'm afraid." I ask him "Can you share your fear with her—tell her about it?" He does that, and Charlotte changes again to the female pillow.

The female says, "I like that. I feel more alive." A red-flag of danger arises in me if she means that she feels more alive *because of* the man. So I say to her, "Be careful about thinking that it is him making you feel alive. This dependency isn't true. You were already alive. Your sadness was alive, even your experience of flatness was an expression of life. You are forgetting to appreciate the details of the flow inside you." Charlotte understands, and I feel a change happening within her—more focus on herself than before.

She shifts to the opposite cushion. The man says he feels more space. He lets himself enjoy this for a few moments.

Charlotte again changes to the female place, and I say to her, "Suppose the man is now able to come and go, and you don't ask any particular behavior from him that will make you feel more alive. Imagine that he has moved toward you and then gone away. Tell me exactly how you feel when he's gone."

She answers, "I feel alone, flat... it is rather like a vacuum..."

I say to her, "You are giving me a perfect description of the feminine nature. I would like you to feel the positive aspect of this being alone, flat and empty. In your words there is a still a negative inflection... in reality, this moment of silence is really beautiful!"

Charlotte remains in silence with her eyes closed, she is looking more deeply into herself. I notice her starting to smile, and then she is laughing: it is enough, after all—this state is just fine. Exactly in this moment she manages to see the value of pure femininity.

Returning to the male cushion, he now finds himself in a confusion. And I know for the first time why he runs. I ask him, "Are you a person who loves freedom?" He nods without speaking. I feel him relaxing, finally, perhaps because he feels understood. It is okay to love freedom.

This session has two significant turning points. The first is where the female comes in touch with her moment as it is, and can recognize that life is not absent: that moment carries her own kind of vitality. Then she no longer falls into the trap of thinking she's alive only when the man is there.

The second important movement in the session happens at the end and is barely visible. Charlotte's male side has always chosen freedom, even though he felt guilty about it, even though he was deeply convinced it was wrong. Now he can drop the guilt. It is not "wrong" for him to refuse to be the woman's source of vitality.

The female part of Charlotte shows well how, in love, the deepest problem for the feminine polarity is self-worth. The cause is connected to the type of energy females have, which is more similar to an empty space than to a substance. The woman is like a receptivity, an awaiting for the male to arrive. When you observe this waiting, this emptiness from a meditative standpoint, it is perfect in itself; it doesn't lack anything in order to be complete.

Sometimes I use a metaphor from chemistry to explain this to my clients. Normally an atom has stability—that is, a nucleus containing a certain number of protons and an equal number of electrons circling around it. The electrons circle in pairs, two in each orbit. But it can happen that an orbit becomes incomplete, which means it has only one of the two electrons that are supposed to be there. Then the atom is ready to acquire another one, which will take the empty place in this valence. And until it comes, the system experiences a sort of restlessness, an instability. The feminine is exactly like the space that awaits a missing electron—she is an expectancy.

If you take a photograph of the atom before its new electron has arrived, you catch it in a moment of instability—but it is beautiful just like that! From a meditator's point of view, this moment in the atom's existence is to be celebrated, even though it misses an electron. There is no need for anything else to happen, the photo is complete in itself.

This is the difference between being identified with need and watching need. If you become identified with the atom's expectation that something is needed to complete it, you will become miserable until the emptiness is filled. If you watch the emptiness as a photographer might, you see it as something beautiful, full of potentiality. In the longing, in the yearning, there is something dynamic that won't be there when the atom is stabilized again and all the action is complete.

In meditation we can enjoy that which has not yet come to a conclusion. When the female is without the male, she's beautiful like that. When the male arrives, she's beautiful in another way. Two photos of these two moments are simply different. If you don't meditate, and you identify with her "lack" in the first moment and her "receiving something" in the second moment, then you will think that the first photo is negative and the second is positive. But if instead you just remain at some distance from the photos and simply observe them both as moments of life, the two will be equal in their beauty.

One polarity with too much power

For the man, things are quite different. His problems come from another angle. The masculine energy has substance—it is not an emptiness—so a male side never feels troubled by aloneness nor by placidness. On the contrary, he likes to stay on his own, and he likes to be active. However, his action is often a "doing." By "doing" I mean he proceeds toward an objective with an idea of *how* to do it. He has a rational plan, and then through his own effort he reaches the goal. He starts to become identified with this ability to move toward an aim and the sense of power that it gives him. Power is, therefore, a thing that he would not like to lose!

This attachment to power has a variety of consequences. One thing I often see in my sessions is that the man has become a dictator, making the woman run night and day, and then he tells me that she never does anything fast enough!

Not always does he use the female's legs to run; sometimes he uses his own. I'm thinking of a particular client, a woman who managed a shop for hardware and interior decoration materials. She started her session by saying, "I'm stressed out, I work long hours, I can't get enough time for myself, not even breaks." It turned out that the male was doing 100% of the job, while the female was in an attitude of "no" and going to sleep. We searched for a more creative choice for the feminine, and we found out that she would like to work with wrought iron making balcony railings. The male side conceded that if she took this job, it would be good for him too. But when it actually came to the moment when he should tell her directly to start, he said, "Don't do it!" I was so surprised! I asked him to explain why, if her choice actually made him feel better. "Well," he admitted, "the real reason is that my sense of power will be reduced, and also my role as a caretaker and protector would go away."

Males like to "do," and they can't stand it when females interrupt them with the need to rest or to just do nothing. For the male side, when he is without action it seems that he doesn't exist.

There is an interesting corollary regarding all this doing: the male side gets approval and recognition from the persons for whom he does things. He can get so addicted to it that he constantly surrounds himself with people who want something done. In this way he keeps himself in action and afterwards receives congratulations. One of my good friends has this sort of inner man. He was preventing the female from having any space, and he was doing this on purpose, he said, so that he would not lose power. He was a man who valued duty, not pleasure, and whenever I talked about the connection between duty and people's praise, he felt himself growing bigger, physically bigger. Because the situation with my friend was informal, I could tease the inner man by saying, "That's your ego which is getting bigger." He laughed.

The male side feels himself to be a force which *goes*. He is afraid that he will lose his power if he relaxes. Yes, it's true that a particular kind of power is lost in relaxation. But then a different sort of power emerges as the relaxation deepens over time. This new power uses the same energy, but its source is "no-mind." Actions still happen but in a different rhythm, and they are more unexpected. There is movement, just as before, but no sense of "I do it," no personal claim. When this sort of creativity arises it comes as an upsurge of energy which acts without regard to the question "how." And its expression is perfectly in tune with the situation. "Let-go" leads to a loss of power in the sense of a domination over one's environment, but it opens up another power, a softer one: the power to touch the environment with love, to be a nourishment.

Don't put yourself in someone else's shoes!

As you have seen, both the masculine and feminine energies have their down sides, but they also have their splendor. And it can happen, when one of them is especially gifted, that it becomes very much admired by the opposite polarity. Sometimes it is the male which is idolized. The female thinks he's so strong, so creative, so active, so able to realize projects in the world that she wants to emulate his behavior. Or, conversely, it can be the female who is the star. The male sees her vast spaciousness, her warm receptivity, her mysterious ability to perceive invisible things, and thinks that this is the way he should be too. In these cases, it is as if the two sides are trying to be united finally by becoming the same in their nature. This is a dangerous mistake, perhaps the most dangerous, because one character will try to efface itself. I have seen it lead to such heavy problems as drug abuse, alcoholism, depression, and anorexia.

Melany was an example. She was rich enough that she didn't have to work, and in the past she had spent whole days lying on the couch smoking hashish so that she wouldn't think or feel. By the time I met her she had begun practicing meditation, so her drug habit was less than before. But she came to me in despair because her daughter didn't want to continue school, and she felt that as a mother she had been a bad example for her daughter—she herself was so unruly.

When I did the resonance check, I found the female quite beautiful and strong—a giver. The male leg was dark, and also the second chakra (regarding work). When a leg is dark like that, it is often a sign of depression, so I asked the male early in the session if he was ever suicidal. He answered that he had thought of it many times.

It turned out that Melany's male was utterly fascinated by the female. Just thinking of her, he became tender and ecstatic. He said to me, "I have so much desire to be a woman. I've never been a woman; up to now I've always been a man." After considering his desire I said, "If you become a woman, the other side of the body won't have a man to relate to. Becoming a woman will not be natural for you; you will have to try, and you will become very tired. So if I were you, I would let go of this idea. If you've always been a man, then *be* a man."

Melany's male was listening too much to advice from the female, how to be more like her: for example, he should not smoke and drink, he should not create shocks, and he should not disturb her pathway. To the female I said, "He smokes and drinks in order to stop the mind, and that's not a bad thing. One could wish for better ways, but the motive is not wrong. He creates shocks because he is not connected to himself. And this happens because of all your 'shoulds.' I believe that he need not concern himself at all about disturbing your pathway; he needs to choose his own pathway. Otherwise there will be imbalance. There are two pathways for a person, and the feminine pathway is not the only one." I warned her against trying to be his teacher. "A woman cannot teach a man to be a man; it is not in the nature of things! Attend to your own business, which is to make yourself happy."

By the end of the session they were each finding their own movements, their own rhythms, and the female enjoyed that his rhythm was faster than hers. For the first time he was not "wrong."

For me, the most amazing moment in the session was when the man said, "I've discovered that when I do what the woman wants at all costs, it's not natural; I have to impose it on myself. And one of the things I impose on myself is the figure of the housewife: to do the best thing for my daughter." This revelation explained to me the darkness in chakra two: the male part was disclosing that the job of perfect mother and housekeeper—which had been his main focus in life for the past 18 years—was not the right job for him. Mystery solved! A small mystery, but nevertheless important in this person's life.

I've seen many instances where one side tries to vacate its place, but this will never work. I am constantly referring to my metaphor, saying that the roving electron and the expectant emptiness that waits for it are both necessary. The feminine should not judge herself as a dead space; rather, she can perceive herself as a vibrant space, capable of welcoming. But with only the feminine energy, things will become too stagnant and life will be boring. There is need for the movement and vitality that the male creates. He knows how to give form, effervescence, playfulness, he knows how to experiment with new paths. He should never be thinking about how to become passive like the female.

Each of them must walk in their own shoes, so to speak. In spite of the old saying, it's not a good idea for one to step into the shoes of the other, not even temporarily.

CHAPTER 9

Job, Money, and Survival Fear

Among the questions that you answered in chapter one, a few were about work. The first of these, addressed to both eyes, was "Are you working?" I ask the question this way because very often, more often than you might suspect, only half of the body is working. It makes no sense to ask further questions to the polarity which is not involved.

Sometimes a polarity that doesn't work is not able to do it because of a strong closure, depression, or history of illness. But usually one of the two polarities simply doesn't want to work. Up to now, it couldn't find any productive activity that would be a pleasure, and so all work is considered something painful, a duty, a condemnation. This polarity is happy to pass the responsibility on to the other—which takes it, but at a price. Each polarity has a natural energy that permits it to earn enough money for one, but not for two. Therefore, every time one part takes on the obligation of earning for two, this part becomes stressed and finally exhausted.

The truth about which part earns and which doesn't

In sessions, I never omit the subject of work even if the client doesn't bring it as a problem. You will remember that in chapter five I said that work, relationship, and meditation are all interconnected as parts of a circle. A disequilibrium will appear in the other two aspects of the circle when one polarity is lazy about work and not aware of the consequences.

And this imbalance shows up frequently in people, because very rarely is the responsibility for work divided in half, 50% for each polarity. The more common proportion is 70% for one side, and 30% for the other side.

To help you get a feeling for how the proportions can vary, I'll give you some examples. If a person has work that requires relating with others and the success of that activity depends on the depth of contact, the feminine side will probably tell me that she does 90% of the work. Then the masculine side will tell me that he is very little involved, maybe 10%. If I have a lawyer as my client, I assume that a large part of the work will be done by the masculine side because it includes rational argument and paperwork. But I shouldn't cling to my assumption because many lawyers take care of their clients from the heart—which requires the abilities of the feminine side.

You can make your own guess about Leonard, the client we met in chapter six. If you remember, he is the designer of car engines using sophisticated computers. His masculine side is the engineer, the solver of problems, so what do you think?—is he doing 100%? Yes, it's true. The feminine is only pushing him and not working herself! Very shortly I am going to introduce Linda, who works in a restaurant. When she was a cook, her two sides were balanced at 50% each. After she was promoted to coordinator she got in trouble, because the male's responsibility increased to 80%, and the female's dropped to 20%.

Whenever I meet an inner couple I try to discern which side is actually taking responsibility for the work—if earning money is necessary. Normally it is the more resonant side. And there are two reasons for this. First, the resonant part is more in contact with its natural inclinations; and second, it is more full of love. This side doesn't even notice when it is carrying more than its share. Typically it will diminish its real contribution to the work, rather than suggest a figure that embarrasses the opposite polarity.

I mention this so that you can understand my next point. Sometimes the two sides are lying when they speak about work. Not that they are lying on purpose, they just don't realize the truth. If I meet an inner couple like Leonard's, where the female has no resonance, she may tell me that she is taking equal responsibility for the work, 50%. And certainly she thinks so! In my opinion, however, she is the one who arranges to have an office space at such a high cost and wants to keep on renting it in the future so that the male cannot stop. She is struggling to keep it and she thinks this is her work, her contribution. For me, this is actually *against* the work. So my figure for her is 0% and I give 100% to the male.

It reminds me of Andreas, another member of the Swedish course where I met Helga. Andreas' problem was that he could never make enough money, even though he worked hard and did many different jobs. Mainly he was a carpenter, but he had various sidelines: special orders from clients, exhibitions of his designs (with another carpenter), and even some graphic design work on the computer. I did an energy check and what I saw was that the female side had a talent for design, so she was giving something positive to the work, but at the moment the male was just in darkness.

When his male and female sat on their two cushions, both expressed that they were working very much. When we looked deeper, it turned out that the male was admiring or perhaps envying the female, and he wanted to be as capable as she. I told him (the male part) that he should go on vacation and let the female take the whole job. He could not believe it! The male part simply did not want to be as small as he actually was. But finally he agreed to stop the effort to have a different size.

When at last the female had the choice of job in her hands, she said she would just create designs. She would drop all things having to do with computer, and especially the boring work of customized orders.

I explained to Andreas and to the group that the quality of presence is what brings money. When a side of you that doesn't have any presence works very hard, it is useless—no matter what efforts you put in, they won't pay off. Andreas' male side thinks he is working 50%, but the truth is, the male's contribution is 10% and the female's is 90%. She is relaxing and he is struggling like a maniac. When it is like this, it is better for the male to relax. After he has rested, his actions will have a different quality.

Earning through relaxation

Once I find out which of the two polarities has the bigger capacity to love, I start investigating what it would really like to be doing. If this part already has a longing for a particular activity—let's say pottery—and is even proficient in it but scared about survival, I often give this little spiel of encouragement:

There are two ways to earn money. One is to give the client what they desire. To do that, first you have to find out their desire and then you have to make a product that satisfies it. When you deliver the product you receive the money, which was your principle objective.

The whole process is not really a pleasure. First you have to calculate how to pay the least possible expenses. Then you have to consider which advertising strategies will persuade the client to give you the most money. And then there is all the "doing" to get the product to happen. At the moment of payment, you feel the client's reluctance to pay: even if you have agreed on a price, he would prefer to pay less. He wants to give you the minimum, so that he has money to satisfy other desires. It's a type of exchange in which the producer and the customer are engaged at the same level—desire. Their interaction, up to and including the last moment, is a subtle fight.

There is another way to earn money. In this one, you don't follow the desire of the client and you are not even searching a client. You do something that gives you joy, and the activity itself is an expression of your love. You would do it even if nobody paid you.

Whoever sees your action, if they have an open heart, will notice the love that is emanating from you as you work. And that person will feel inspired to support the existence of such a quality. They want it to go on living, because it is not so common in this world. Sometimes they support you by purchasing your product even if they don't really need it. But more often the support is indirect. You might be offered a free place for your vacation, or tools and materials that you need for renovating your house. Or perhaps you get paid for something which was not your job, but which you did as a favor. Whatever the person gives you is accompanied by their joy to give it. They never want to give you less, in fact they wish they could give you more!

In this way of gaining money you are paid for just being, and not for what you do. This is something very different than you will ever hear about in the normal business world. In this way of living you don't exactly earn money, but the money arrives to you as a gift. And in the same way, your work was a gift to existence, not motivated by any further purpose than the creativity itself.

So ends the little speech I use to help a character explore the idea that work can be something relaxing, not an effort. But these words only succeed in helping the person to jump if a creative impulse is already there. For example, with Maya. She was a full-time school teacher, but she wanted to turn her house into a bed & breakfast. She took the jump—reduced school teaching to a bare minimum and put her energy into finding guests. I suggested to her to have Family Constellation groups in her attic, where there is a large, comfortable room, and now she is fully successful as a group organizer, cook, and hospice manager. Maya is blissed out by the change that happened to her regarding work.

It is more difficult when someone cannot believe yet in this new possibility—for example Alex. He has been working in an office in the city because he thinks that you can only make money in a city. When we explore together what he would like to do, we discover that he likes to travel. Also he likes to talk to people from other cultures. He has a penchant for luxury items—from fancy watches to antique cars. For me it is easy to imagine which sorts of work could include all these elements, but Alex is simply not able to believe that money can come from an activity he likes. He is so conditioned to think that work is tiring, unpleasant, and that it consists in doing what other people want.

We are wrongly educated about work, so we always start our career with the wrong question. Instead of "What would I like to do?" we occupy ourselves with the question "How can I earn?" This question about "how" is from the head, not the heart. Rationally we study the history, we observe how other people have earned money in the past. And then we start our efforts to copy someone else's idea, to mechanically repeat what has been done before. It can never be fresh this moment, never innovative, and never satisfying. Only drudgery.

Almost everyone has wrong work, disconnected from their

own roots. When people begin to meditate, slowly they realize that they are not happy with the work they do and as a consequence they change their work after some time. Maybe this is one of the reasons why the society has become suspicious whenever you talk about meditation. It certainly will disturb the social order if so many people change their jobs!

But the real problem is not that. The real problem is that you cannot answer the question "What would I like to do?" You are not in touch with your natural flow, neither in the masculine polarity nor in the feminine. You are cluttered inside; the channels are filled with debris, so you don't find clear water.

The channels can be opened again with many different therapy methods. But therapy will only bring its full benefit if you also become a meditator. Therapy helps to go through and to abandon the repressions of the past, to clear negative emotions, but it doesn't necessarily put you in touch with your positive resources. Meditation, on the other hand, relaxes you and helps you to see the difference between personality and your essential being, and to disidentify with the part of yourself still connected to desires.

When your system starts to relax in meditation, one polarity in you will be attracted to doing through non-doing. One part, male or female, will notice that in relaxing, things happen by themselves. You should listen to that part of you and the skeptical part, which doesn't trust, should be ignored for a while. In this way, the part which flows will begin to discover work that has magic in it. The more you make yourself available for this work, the more you find yourself involved in creativity rather than productivity. Productivity has a desired end, while creativity is an end in itself.

Creativity dissolves the fear of death

Creativity is different from what people think it is. They imagine that it is a kind of artwork: painting or sculpture or design. Or if the category is extended to other arts, then music, photography, filmmaking and dance can be included. But actually this is a misunderstanding. Anything can be creative. It depends on the quality you bring to the activity.

Even eating can be creative—it depends on how you eat. You can eat in a mechanical way, thinking about other things, just shoving food into the body so that you don't feel empty. Then you won't get any pleasure from the activity of eating, only from the full stomach afterward.

Or you can be present while you eat, letting the hands rest while you chew, noting how it feels after you have swallowed a bite and for a split second you are doing nothing at all. And then some "mysterious" force lifts your hand from its resting place and takes it... where? It is this flowing toward an unexpected outcome that makes something creative. Your hand is at rest and you don't know what it is going to do next. You watch, intensely interested in the unknown future: what will happen?

Just let yourself be surprised. The hand goes to the fork, or to the glass, or to the bread, or to the knife, or to the napkin, or to the serving dish... You think that your next bite is going to be zucchini but it turns out to be spaghetti—the hand went there by itself. This is the process I call "doing through non-doing." Certainly something happened, but you cannot say "you" did it. "You" were thinking to eat veggies and pasta happened instead.

This is a small example, just to let you know that ordinary moments can be creative. But creativity can also happen in any job where you are alert, available to the unknown. You plan to do one thing and you notice that something completely different happens. And afterwards you realize that you invented something new, or at least did an old thing in a new way.

The feeling inside when you are creative is of being in contact with a breeze, a spirit-wind. Sometimes it's a very soft breeze, almost imperceptible unless you are listening for it. And sometimes it is strong and you feel whipped along by a gale. The breeze is carrying you like it carries a leaf, dancing you like it dances a leaf.

Whenever you are carried by the breeze, you will have a sense of freedom simultaneously. Perhaps you have already known this freedom before, riding on the sea while the breeze is carrying your boat along. There is no feeling of restraint anywhere, and at the same time you are at rest.

Creativity and freedom are very connected. But just as people have a wrong idea about creativity, they have a wrong idea about freedom. Most people think freedom is to be able to acquire whatever you desire: you can buy any yacht you want; you can travel to any city you want and whenever you want; you can have any partner you want, and change on a moment's notice. But if you look closer at this so-called freedom, you'll notice that you have to take care of a yacht after you buy it, or otherwise pay the maintenance man; you'll have to involve yourself with ticket agencies and hotels when you travel, and things go wrong sometimes; and if you leave a string of angry women behind you, energetically you will feel heavy, not free. So as far as I can see, this kind of freedom will bring only headaches!

No, freedom is something completely different. If you know what is creativity, you know the taste of freedom. In creativity you are ready for the unknown. I don't mean that there are no future plans, no priorities, no goals. Of course, you generally have a frame for the future—that the body needs to sleep tonight and to cook something tomorrow, that you need a house to sleep in and clothes to wear. But I am speaking about the small, small moment that is now—you don't know exactly what is going to happen in it. You watch. And something happens. And this thing happens without effort.

Effortlessness is the ground of creativity and freedom both. When I'm demonstrating how to put a sweater in a closet effortlessly, people will say, "Yes, we can see that when you wrap the sweater around your neck, you do something original. We can see that it happened from spontaneous impulse, not plan. But how can you call that freedom? It seems you are limited to only one action in that moment, when there are thousands of other choices for using the same moment in other ways."

Yes, to the mind it seems like a limitation, that you do only that thing which happens by itself. And in each moment, if you relax, only one thing happens! So it seems like one thing gained and a thousand things missed. But deep inside your being you'll find a different perspective. You'll find that the one thing which did happen, out of all those other possibilities, was the perfect thing for that moment, for the particular circumstances of the present moment. And you couldn't have thought of such a perfect movement, such a perfect response—so genuine, so funny. You are glad the breeze did it, and you could rest.

Resting in such a way, you feel very big. Bigger than the body, bigger than when you are surrounded by mind and its desires. You feel connected to some ineffable bigness. You feel endless, without limits. Freedom, in other words, is freedom from your small "self." Your self, your own mind, was the only imposition, the only imprisonment.

What does this mean, that you are an imposition to yourself? I'll give you an example that is perhaps quite universal. You work in an office and you notice that your job doesn't please you so much—many times during the day you have this sensation. If you think to leave the job, immediately a fear grows inside you: then, how will I survive? Because of this idea, this fear, you decide not to listen to any impulse for change... and you return, mechanically, day after day to the office.

You are still holding on to many ideas that you heard repeatedly over the years: "One cannot always do what one wants to do... And don't believe that other jobs will be any better than this one... All jobs are basically the same..." Now, as you use these things as excuses to support your staying in that office, the only thing remaining for you is to "feel" less so that it will be less painful. You shrink yourself, and still you don't look directly at the fear. And what is it? The fear about survival—the fear that the body will die. And in this way that you have chosen, you are already dying, shrinking, bit by bit.

If you were to start to meditate, to flow from one unplanned thing to the next, you would discover that the body survives. You have to experiment, you have to try it. Then you will see that when love is flowing, people help you. In relaxation, the body survives until the right moment for it to die. And in that moment a meditator will observe the separation of the being from the body in exactly the same way he has been observing his hand move to the fork. He will be effortless in the same way as he is when he watches a gesture or a breath. Relaxation in life becomes relaxation in death.

And this is the strange side effect that goes with a more total expression of one's own nature: the fear about survival disappears because you understand that the moments of life and the moments of death are not all that different.

Taking responsibility for work

"She" is not really a mechanic

Davide has been a social acquaintance of mine for one year, and so I already know that he works for a heavy equipment company in Verona, Italy, and is responsible for the repair of trucks, tractors, and earth-moving machines. He supervises other mechanics and jumps into the actual work whenever they can't manage.

Today he arrives to the session very agitated—in fact, he has put his back out for no reason in particular. He tells me that his company has just offered him a new job. It would be a step up in his career, but he would have to move to another location and this creates an inner conflict. On the one hand, the offer is a good one. On the other hand, in this last year he has had such positive experiences in Verona—a new girlfriend, buying and renovating his own flat and moving in with her, making many new friends that he likes—that he is very reluctant to change location.

Davide says that his relation with the girlfriend is good—except in situations like the present one, when he doesn't want advice. He is afraid he will get lost and never know what *he* wants to do.

We start with the resonance check. The female side is much more resonant than I expected, and I realize that it has grown rapidly this past year because of the girlfriend's loving influence. Davide's female is delicate, sensitive, and she loves light. She is happy to sit in a corner full of plants and feel the sunrays coming in through the window. My first thought was, "This woman is not a mechanic! Wrong job. And she's full of strength now, she should be working."

Next, the right foot. The male is not resonant at all. His movements are plodding, as if he has to walk through thick mud. He has to keep on going, rain or shine; he is dogged, heavy, and I hear him sigh and start again, putting his shoulder to the rock like Sisyphus.

The rest of the resonance check is normal—some resonance but not in all of the chakras.

I use the blindfold first, asking Davide to cover one eye at a time. The female (through the left eye) answers my question by saying she is not working right now, she is not involved in the job. Would she like to be involved in some other work of her choice?—she doesn't know. Does she think women shouldn't have to work?—no, women can work. I propose to her that with the job situation right now, she has to be absent eight hours of the day and she could actually have those eight hours back to do what she likes with them.

The male side, on the contrary, *is* working. He's not especially satisfied but it's not so bad, he says. When I ask if he could allow her to do a job, to use some of the hours in her own way, he says he would have to control whether she was making enough money. I propose to him that perhaps he could let her work and then do his mechanics part-time, for example with Formula One. Surely he could make money at this also, and then the timings would be more flexible.

When we set up the pair I am interested to see that the woman, who I perceived as very much stronger than the man, is pretending to be a baby. The man, who I considered weak, is pretending to be her papa or "nonno" (grandfather). He is taking care of her materially, he says, "but she doesn't need much." I say, "We are conditioned to think this is love, but it's not love. I recommend that you stop taking responsibility for her: you are taking her legs away."

When I go back to the female side, we look together for things she would like to do. The only details she can be clear about are "It's with people, many people, and I'm talking to them but not about work." I ask her, do you want to move to Perugia or Bologna (the two places of the new job offer)? She says, "Could be okay. The place is not really important."

Then some surprises. She actually does like cars. She actually does some work in the present job: she has good rapport with her subordinates, and she gets creative ideas when there is some problem to be solved. She doesn't feel either of these contributions as "work," but they are! "Then do you choose to stay in the same work with heavy equipment?" I ask. Again she answers, "I don't know."

Speaking to Davide in the witnessing chair, we agree that the female simply doesn't want to take any responsibility. So I decide to do only one thing more and then leave it so. I suggest that the male ask her directly to take back her own responsibility—this is for his own practice, to hear himself say the sentences and feel okay saying them. When he does that, the female is definitely listening. "Look," I say to her, "being a baby is fun. But it's even more fun to have legs. It's the same good feeling as having your own flat, which you told me you enjoy so much. When you have a creativity that's your own, you gain a sense of dignity and self-worth." The woman says she will have to try it out, and she is surprised to feel no fear.

Without any real resolution to Davide's question of whether he should change his job, we return to more neutral positions, with Davide facing me from the witnessing chair. I ask, "Do you have any new view about the question you brought?" He says, "The question isn't answered, but it's changed. Now the question is, can this new offer serve the needs that I have on both sides of me? The new job has a bigger role as a supervisor. It has more sales work, and so more contact with customers. And it has less work as a mechanic. The man could work less and enjoy a promotion, which would make his mind happy. But the main difference I feel now is that *I* will decide, it won't be somebody else's decision, but mine."

Sometimes it's interesting to know what happens after the session. Six months later, Davide told me that he hadn't accepted the new job. In the end, Bologna wasn't possible so there was only the option of Perugia that was too far away for him. But the big news was that

THE TWO SHORES OF LOVE

Davide has begun to search for work in a completely different field: sophisticated hi-fi equipment, which has long been his passion.

Now you can read about another session which deals with responsibility on the job.

Testing oneself in the kitchen

Linda oversees the kitchen in a restaurant. Until a few months ago, she was a cook there and enjoyed a close relationship with the other cooks. Her problem is that when her role changed to that of manager, she felt some of the other people turn against her. And after a while she started to respond to their antagonism in a like manner, also aggressive.

The resonance check shows resonance in the female, and high sensitivity. She has no need to prove herself, but she likes to just "be." The male has the anger Linda was talking about. It is as if some other person attacks first, and he feels compelled to fight back. There is a picture of a fighting fist in chakra two (job chakra), resonance in chakra three (which means successful supervision of others), and resonance in the heart and the top of the head. My guess, even before we proceed, is that when Linda was cook, she did the job more from her female side and, having switched to coordinator, now she does it more from the male.

Questioning the two eyes about jobs, I learn that both sides were equally involved in cooking, but in the present job of coordinator, the male is taking 80% of the load and the female only 20%. So I am right in guessing that the male's involvement has gone up.

Now I am going to briefly summarize the rest of the session, mentioning only the high points so that you can understand the resolution to Linda's concern.

Step 1: Setting up the pair. We establish the female polarity first. Then the male, looking back at her, sees her as stupid and frivolous. The female sees the male as rigid and weak and needing her help—which she can't or doesn't want to give. Hence, judgments from both sides are damaging the inner relationship.

Step 2: Supporting the male. I spend the bulk of the session time helping the male to become free of the female's judgments and to receive love and support from other sources. The female actually appreciates his new independence. But I tell him to watch out, because she is picky, fussy. "She likes you when you are true to yourself, but you can't be that way all the time. In a weaker moment, when you're not present, she won't like you. You'll go crazy if you absorb any of her judgments, positive or negative."

Step 3: Finding his own activities. I explain to the male that if he wants to trust himself and to believe that he is a loving person, he should carry out only those aspects of the job that he really likes doing; then he can be sure that love is flowing, and no one's criticism can shake his self-assurance. He says that the aspects he likes are ordering supplies and stocking the food dispensary, driving the van for pick-ups, and doing things together with the other people. And the aspects he no longer wants responsibility for are the menu and the overview of staff schedules and productivity.

Step 4: Increasing the female's responsibilities. I say to the female that if she wants the male to keep his self-confidence and independence, these last two responsibilities are now on her. She can choose to take them, or to quit this job or to change it. She says she wants to keep the job and take them on. She doesn't want to decide the menu alone, so she will choose another person from the crew to help her (she says the name of that person). And for the overview, she wants to do it in a different way—she wants the crew members to be responsible for themselves. She tells me that if she takes on these two parts of the job, each side will be carrying 50%.

Step 5: Defining the source of the error. I ask the female why she did not make this change earlier. She says that she didn't trust herself. Probably her way of supervising the kitchen staff will not meet the approval of her superiors; they may not understand it.

Step 6: My insight. I remind Linda of a phrase we used in describing the female: that she doesn't need to prove herself, but likes to just "be." In this case, she actually *needs* to prove herself! She has to endure the "knocks" that responsibility brings. "Of course when you do things your own way, there are always people who criticize. And sometimes you even have to leave a job because of your convictions. But in this way you mature and become self-reliant." Linda's female will have to follow this path if she wants the inner man to unclench his fist and develop a strength that is not tense but relaxed.

CHAPTER 10

Past Lives

If you are a very rational person and you only like things that are demonstrable, don't read this chapter. There is no scientific proof that people have had other lives before this, nor can there be.

But I have experienced energies connected to past lives, both in myself and in other people, which I felt to be true. Very often such memories from the distant past were imprinted by dramatic experiences, and particularly by painful ones. Because of my interest in these phenomena I gradually stumbled upon ways to repair the damage caused in the past by reviewing those experiences which are still having a disruptive effect upon the present.

To explain to you how this repair can happen, I have to share things which are even more mysterious. If you really can't tolerate mysterious things, don't read further! This is my second warning!

These mysterious things have to do with the relation between an enlightened master and his disciples. I'm speaking of Osho, because he is the enlightened man I have met personally. But I'm sure it is the same with other masters too, provided they are the real thing. The disciple—otherwise known as a *sannyasin* or seeker of truth—has a conditioned personality the same as everybody else, but he chooses to relate to an enlightened person—in my case Osho—because the presence of the master nourishes his being. Whenever the disciple finds something which carries the fragrance of the master he will be sure it has truth, or is connected to the truth. I'm going to use this principle when I describe two past-life sessions later on. But for now, I only wish to share my experience: that a master keeps me in line with my truth, precisely because his being and my being are the same.

Previous traumas can affect you now

I want to talk about a massage group that I conducted recently. Normally people think that massage is not such a powerful tool as psychotherapy. But in fact, every time the group is practicing massage of the legs, many persons experience emotions which are very deep and difficult to manage.

It was the last day of the group. We had finished massaging the legs in the morning, and at the start of the afternoon session we were dancing to some very strong music. I noticed that Isabella was weeping, so I stopped the music and asked the members of the group to be present with her. She was leaning on a pile of mattresses and we were scattered on the floor at her feet. Isabella told us, through her tears, that her body seemed to be divided in two parts, and that she couldn't feel the lower part—the legs and feet.

I knew what her problem was (sorry—another irrational thing). Isabella had been burned as a witch in a past life. Certainly she didn't realize that she was in good company: she was one of about five million women burned alive in the Middle Ages. I said to her, "Death is not the problem, because when nature takes your body, you surrender yourself. But when somebody else has the power to take away your body, you rebel against power—their power to damage and destroy. But people do such things! So what can help you in that moment is to feel contact and connection with some other loving people who surround you."

THE TWO SHORES OF LOVE

After guiding her into remembering this episode of her past life, I asked her to make eye contact with the group members one by one and to tell each person how she is feeling after the public condemnation to death. To the first person she said, "I feel fear." To another, "I feel alone." To a third, "I am without hope." And then, as she continued, I invited the people to tell her in return how they would feel if someone were going to take their body. And, one at a time, they told her, "If someone had intention to take away my body I would feel outraged," or "I would feel guilty." When she came to me, I said, "I remember when I, too, was accused by the court, and there was defiance in me... I remember being defiant." Just knowing that someone else had actually had the same experience made Isabella feel less alone.

Then I asked her to see the thing from a wider point of view, that she had lost a body but now she had a new one, and one day she would lose this body and get another one. I said to her, "Please enter again into the picture of your past life and observe how attached you are to that particular body that you had. Once more, tell to each person about your desire to keep precisely this one." So she said first, "I want to keep this body, it's marvelous," then "It's beautiful," then "I want to keep this body because it's *my* body." This word 'my' was the key to help her see something more. I told her about one of my favorite sentences from Osho, when he said, "Nothing can be called 'mine' except consciousness." And Isabella relaxed... in fact, bodies, like relationships, come and go. I asked her if it would be okay to continue dancing—to celebrate *this* present body, which was the only one which could dance right now. Putting on the music, I said, "This is for all the witches in the group, including Enrico!"—and I played *Diavolo in me* (The Devil in Me) from Zucchero.

A second chance

Two days later, the Enrico just mentioned came to me for an individual session—prearranged, I ought to say, before there was any witch-music. He spoke about a fear that sometimes paralyzed him. When I made the resonance check, I was sure that his fear came from a past life. My perception was that something shocking had happened to him quite suddenly: his life at that time had been going forward smoothly, peacefully, when all of a sudden things went wrong.

Enrico, by chance, already knew which past life was involved, so he told me about it. He had been a traveling artist in Europe moving from city to city with a group of friends. He was happy, he was free. And in a certain moment, when he was driving his cart in a forest, he was stopped by an angry crowd who told him that he was possessed by the devil, and these people had killed him.

Even if regarding past lives you can never say exactly when things took place, I presume that this happened during the Middle Ages. I asked Enrico, "Have you any idea how they killed you?" He told me he was feeling pain in his throat just then, so probably it had something to do with his neck.

Enrico was a sannyasin, so I decided to use a technique I know for reframing the past. I asked him to go back in time to the moment just before he was accused, because we have need of Osho's presence in that moment to repair the trauma. Enrico said, "I'm seated on a wagon pulled by two horses. I'm alone, the people have not yet arrived." I asked Enrico to see if Osho appears in this situation—as a light, as a presence, or in his physical body with his robe and his hat. Enrico said, "He's there, I can see him physically." I asked him if Osho is seated in the vehicle with him. Enrico said, "I am in the wagon. He is below, standing on the ground next to the wheel."

SP: Now that Osho is there, you simply relax. The story will unfold by itself, and you just watch if anything happens differently because you are aware of Osho's presence.

Enrico: Now the people have arrived, about fifteen of them, both men and women. This time they cannot enter into the wagon because Osho is standing exactly in the spot where they climbed up before. His presence is preventing them. So they go away. I'm amazed! Now Osho gets into the cart and seats himself to my left, and we go our own way.

SP: A person with love has a need to share it, particularly a man, otherwise he becomes weak. In this case you were sharing it with Osho, and it was very difficult then for the people to harm you.

(Enrico was listening.)

SP: The position of Osho to your left in the wagon is significant. It's the place of the feminine. Did you have a girlfriend in that life?

Enrico: No. I loved freedom very much, and I wouldn't have been able to move around if I had a woman.

SP: Were you afraid of the responsibility for children?

Enrico: No, more the fear of being tied to a house.

SP: You have the idea that all women want to tie you down. I know there are many who would do that, but maybe you can let Osho choose one for you that won't suffocate you. They exist!

Enrico: Yes, I can see now a woman who is traveling with me.

SP: Then it would have been impossible for the crowd to kill you. It's almost impossible to carry away half of a couple when love is flowing between the two persons. Love is a sort of protection.

My feeling is that Enrico's problem will be completely resolved in this life, because now he has a girlfriend he loves very much, one who leaves him in freedom—so the same thing can't happen again.

But it was necessary for him to go into the past, remember the trauma, understand something new about it, and repair the damage created at that time. Otherwise the line between the past and the present remains fractured, and the subconscious continues to react to present situations with old information. Now Enrico's past and present have been realigned, joined into one continuum.

I believe that the whole story of the witches being burned to death in the Middle Ages was a conflict between male and female energies. The masculine was powerful as far as the world was concerned, politically powerful. But the feminine was more powerful in a different way. The representatives of the Church were fundamentally male, and they could smell a certain vibration belonging to those people, now called "sensitives," whose interior silence made them capable of perceiving non-physical things. This vibration was denounced as "dangerous to the society" and the people who had it, such as Enrico, were destroyed—in his case not by the Church but by the general populace. That's why, when I played *Diavolo in me*, I said it was also for Enrico, even though he's a man. According to me, he has the same "dangerous" vibration.

Not to repeat mistakes

The hermit

A sannyasin, Gabriela, comes to me for a problem about relationship: her boyfriend wants to separate, and she refuses to accept it. And by chance she has brought the boyfriend with her to my house, so I get to meet him even before the session starts.

When I do the resonance check I see a picture of an inner man quite different than the actual boyfriend, so at first I think she has chosen a wrong partner. Her inner man is very strong, spiritually developed; whenever he wants something he is very direct in asking for it. He is also physically strong, with a very loud voice. Her boyfriend, by contrast, is quiet, frail and thin, not talkative. Because of the extreme discrepancy, I do the reading of her two feet for a second time and by then it is clear to me that the quality of Gabriela's actual partner is the same as her inner woman's.

When I tell Gabriela about the strength I find in her inner man, she tells me that in her past life she was a hermit—meaning that in that life she was a man. He was quite accustomed to living alone, and he was never bored by it.

I set up the pair, with the inner man and inner woman sitting on chairs, facing each other. The woman admires the man tremendously, she puts him on a pedestal—and I can understand because he is really a strong character in every sense. She feels herself inferior to him.

While she speaks, the feminine side reminds me of people that I met in East Berlin before the Wall came down. So I ask her if she has ever lived in a communist country. She answers yes, that her father was Romanian. She was born in Romania and lived there for twenty-two years.

I ask her to close her eyes, to remember the place where she grew up, and to see if between the ages of 0 and 22 she can manage to find a moment when Osho was present with her in that place. She answers no, she doesn't find him there. So I tell her to go before her birth, and look for him in the interval between the end of the last life and the beginning of this one. This time she says yes, he's there. I say to her, "Tell Osho that you are about to incarnate in Romania, that you are choosing Romania, and listen for his response." She tells me that Osho is saying, "You can do it, but I'm not agreeing with your choice." I ask Gabriela's female, "Do you follow his advice?" She says, "No, I don't want to listen."

We change over to the male side, because I want to know if the masculine part was able to communicate with the feminine part in that particular moment. I found out that the inner man had said nothing, because he wanted the woman to do as she pleased. I ask the man if, in this moment between the end of the last life and the beginning of this one, Osho is present for him. He answers no. That means we will have to go back into the previous incarnation, to know what has interrupted his connection with the master.

The inner man tells me, "In that life, I died in a terrible way. I fell in a hole in the forest and, because I was living alone, there was absolutely no one to help me." I ask him if Osho is there with him in the hole. He says no. I ask him if there was any preceding moment in that life when he could meet Osho. He says, "Yes, there was a time when he was present. I had a wife and she got pregnant. I freaked out and left her when the child was not yet born. I couldn't imagine involving myself in a situation like that because to me it wasn't spiritual. That's when I became a hermit, living by myself."

I ask him to stay for a moment in that situation before he left the woman. If he is near to her, he should tell me how his body is placed relative to hers. He says, "The woman is standing and I am sitting down." I tell him to relax and Osho will direct all events that are to follow... he should just relax as if he's watching a movie. He exclaims in amazement, "Osho is telling me to stay with the family. I see the child being born and I see that love is growing!" These words are pronounced with unexpected pleasure.

I tell him, "The choice you made before was an error, and the consequence is that you fell into a hole. Now you can make this new choice. This time we don't know how you will die in the end, but certainly it will be different than starvation. Now, move forward in time once again to the interval between that death and the next life and see if you want to communicate with the inner woman your preference for where to incarnate." He says, directly to her, "I want to tell you that I prefer Germany."

Gabriela changes to the opposite chair. I ask the female side, "What happens in you when he says he wants to be born in Germany?" She says, "It's very new to feel so much connected to him. I would like to trust, but right now I trust only 90%. I have fear that what happened before will be repeated."

Change over. The male part says to her, "It was a terrible death, being alone in a hole without food and water. You can be absolutely sure that I will never do it again!" Change over. She says, to me, "He is getting smaller. I'm growing bigger. But he's still a little bigger than me." Change over. He says, again directly to her, "I've made a very big mistake. I'm really sorry." Change over. She says, to me, "Now we are the same size. I choose to go with him to Germany."

I ask her, "Why did you choose Romania before?" She answers, "Because the communist idealism represented the possibility to have a family—I never had one, because he left me. I liked the idea of a family where everyone was equal. Only now I can understand what Osho was trying to tell me about my idealism: that I have canceled all the spiritual work that I did previously."

I ask Gabriela to sit on the chair of the witness, thinking we have come to the end of the session. But then another question pops into my head, and I have to speak to the two sides separately again. This time I use the eyepatch to cover one eye at a time. I ask both sides if they want to continue living in the present location, and both say no. I ask if they want to remain with the present boyfriend. They both say no.

So now there is a clarity regarding Gabriela's original question about whether she should stay in the relationship. Something that was creating a tension before has been unblocked.

Other people are mirrors

In speaking of the feminine and masculine aspects, it is important to recognize the influence that the distant past has on you. You are older than the life you are living now. You were not born as a "tabula rasa," as many psychological theories maintain, and it wasn't your parents who formed your personality. My vision is the opposite. I think that each of us has developed his own characteristics over a very long period, over ages and ages, and we choose parents and other significant partners because they can suitably mirror these characteristics. This is not necessarily a conscious choice. It can happen in the period before birth that you are attracted to incarnate in a certain situation, as if you belong there. As you grow up, this situation will then function as a mirror. It will show you parts of yourself—in your parents, in your friends, acquaintances, other family members, and later on in your husband or your wife or your partner.

Naturally, the parents have the biggest influence as far as repeating those behaviors which are familiar to you. But it's important to see that they are not the cause of who you are. If you think they are the cause, you will be in a position of impotence. If you understand that *you* are the cause of a situation, you can do something—you can change yourself. And the change that you make on the inside takes you to more consciousness, to more relaxation. You will see immediately that the external mirror gives a different presentation of the very same people who used to trigger a reaction in you. Sometimes it is the parents who change, and sometimes it is your perception of them that alters.

Returning to Gabriela, she has made a shift inside during this session. When she goes home, the "mirror" will show something new. Her boyfriend may change, in the sense that different aspects of him may come to the surface and other aspects of him that were visible before may recede into the background. Gabriela's new energy will change her perspective of the boyfriend. That's why, even though both sides of her expressed a preference not to be with him anymore, we cannot say right now what the future will bring.

CHAPTER 11

A Dialogue is Possible

Early on I proposed to you a simple experiment in which you could meet your two polarities and feel their qualities. Perhaps their responses to the ten questions were so different that you could already see possible sources of conflict, but we were not yet ready to contend with difficulties.

In this chapter I will give you a similar exercise in which the two parts express themselves through the eyes, but this time we find out more about their relationship. Specifically, we observe whether they have made themselves dominant or submissive, one to the other, and whether in the end there is a proposal for loosening any bondage they have created.

Uncovering dependency

For this experience, I suggest that you first be the listener to someone else's male and female sides, so that you understand well how the exercise works. Afterwards you can do it yourself, and you'll be more relaxed because you won't need to guide your assisting partner simultaneously. Speaking of partners, I strongly recommend that you don't choose your girlfriend or boyfriend. With them, you are too involved to be a neutral listener... and naturally there is the same problem in reverse!

You—now the listener—ask the person to cover one eye with a blindfold, and for convenience in my explanation, ask them to cover the right eye. Their left eye is now open, which is the window to the feminine side. Looking into the left eye, you will see that you are meeting a female "person" in front of the actual eye (an outgoing energy), or behind the eye (a withdrawn energy), or precisely in the center of the eye. You tell your partner exactly where you are meeting the female, and then she answers the following four questions.

1. What qualities do you find in yourself when you have eye-contact with the listener? Start with your feelings at the moment of meeting, and then go on to describe your characteristics in general.

2. Which activities in your life bring you into a space of creativity or love?

3. Do you take care of your material survival by means of your own interests?

4. Do you have any dependencies, in the sense that you lean on someone?

After the female has answered the questions, you (as listener) make a summary out loud about what kind of person you have just met. Use only two or three sentences, and the female can adjust or correct your summary because perhaps she didn't tell you everything about herself.

Now your friend can close the left eye and rest a little. You change the blindfold so that the right eye can open and see out.

Then you ask the same questions to the masculine side, and at the end again make a summary.

Now you are going to talk to the two sides once more, but this time asking only two questions. In these questions, there is a reference to the opposite side. If the person can't remember how is the opposite side, jog their memory with the summary. Start with the feminine side (the right eye is covered).

5. Do you have enough space in your life to express your creativity and do things in your own way? Or do you feel overrun, dominated by the man who you just heard speaking?

6. Do you manage the other person? Do you direct, advise, control, or dominate him? Do you want him to be different?

Change the blindfold to the other eye. And ask the same questions to the masculine side.

7. Do you have enough space in your life to express your creativity and do things in your own way? Or do you feel overrun, dominated by the woman who you just heard speaking?

8. Do you manage the other person? Do you direct, advise, control, or dominate her? Do you want her to be different?

After answering from both the masculine and feminine sides, the partner removes the blindfold and from now on, you as the listener take the active role until the end of the exercise.

Let yourself imagine that these two "persons" meet each other at a party and in time they become a couple. You can now tell your partner your fantasy of what kind of life these two will have together—how their future will unfold. Of course it is only your projection, but perhaps your partner will laugh in recognition of the pattern that you predict.

Most probably both polarities are in desire; they think that everything is going well as it is, and they don't want to change anything. But you can see that they are missing air, missing freedom. Try to decide which polarity seems the closest to tasting freedom, and then tell your partner which one you choose. The partner puts the blindfold on again, covering one eye and leaving the chosen eye open. You are going to talk to this part, you are going to tell this person (male or female) your vision of how it might look if they were free. But remember, it needs to be convincing. You have to make freedom sound very inviting and persuade the person into letting go of the comfort and coziness of dependency!

If the person expresses reluctance to be free, then just respect that. At this point you can stop. It is enough that one part hears about a new possibility, even if they cannot say yes to it right now.

By chance it may happen that this part is already free. This polarity will certainly tell you if he or she is already living the vision you propose. Then you change the blindfold to the other side and talk to the second polarity, asking how this part feels when the first one is free. They will tell you about the struggle they are going through, finding the way to their own individuality, while the other side has managed to do it more quickly!

Creating harmony in the inner relationship

The exercise that you just did was meant to give some encouragement to the inner couple—first to your partner's and then to yours, if you tried it for yourself, too. I hope you were pleasantly surprised by your own potential. My purpose was not to teach you how to improve anyone else's inner relationship. I ask you to understand that other techniques belonging to the Star Sapphire method may eventually be needed before the male and female come into harmonious accord. But at least you can see that it's possible.

Now I am going to give some samples in which the two parts of a person melt into deeper love for each other. First I will tell you about a woman who feels guilty when she relaxes!

The lady at a party

Francesca, who is Italian, has taken sessions from me before. For years she taught English in a public school in Naples, and after becoming a meditator she discovered that she didn't like it anymore. But she could not let go of teaching because of fear about survival, so she reduced that work to part-time in order to have a minimum but steady income and then permitted herself to take on other projects that she liked. Recently she has opened a meditation center with seven other people, and all of the eight associates work there for free. Now the others have asked her to be responsible for the therapy groups that happen in the center. She is already organizing two long training courses each year, separate from the center, for which she receives payment.

Today, Francesca tells me that her inner state is not good. Five days after the center opened she started to feel a tension in her throat and chest, and a feeling of being trapped. "It is like being in prison," she reports. Also she has some questions about her relationship, which has been going through a difficult period.

When I do the resonance check I notice that the feminine side, which in the past has always been joyous and overflowing, today feels bleak and without much life. I think to myself, this must be the person who is feeling trapped. The masculine side used to be weaker, but today it is the more vibrant of the two. I conclude that it is on its own correct path. It is not very resonant, but more so than last time and it is sufficiently flowing.

I decide to set up the pair, and Francesca enters first into her masculine side. When I describe him I use the word 'self-possessed'. The feeling is that he takes decisions, that he makes choices, and whether they are right or wrong he stands by them. He is working in the center and I see him trying to see the whole picture, to have the overview.

Changing over to the second cushion, Francesca (now as the female) describes the man as a good person who at the moment is quite active. But the female tells me that she is interfering with him, watching all his movements, introducing doubt as to whether he is doing the right things. She doesn't criticize him exactly, but she continuously indicates her opinion about each of his movements.

Back on the first cushion, the male looks at the female and finds her closed right now. He says her eyes are looking at him but they are saying, "Don't come closer." He would like to connect but can't, and he doesn't know why she's closed—saying this, he is starting to cry.

When I ask the female why she is concerned with his movements and not with her own, she says she feels some kind of revenge—as if she is getting back at someone by refusing to be interested in herself anymore.

We return to the male side. I ask him, "What do you think this revenge is about?"

Francesca (male): Ah, now I can see it. She has been put in a place where she doesn't want to be. The location we chose for the meditation center has buildings all around, and there is no sun—it is too much for her. Actually, she needs to be in contact with nature. And she's in a way reacting by depriving herself of that more and more. Even when she has time to go for a walk by the sea—and she loves it—she denies herself this pleasure.

Change over.

Francesca (female): Yes, it is me who feels trapped. If I have to suffer, then I will suffer *fino in fondo*, all the way.

SP: Well, if you had been in contact with this need to have more nature around and to not be in that location, you could have said no. You could have said, "I don't involve myself in this location." Why you didn't say no?

Francesca (female): Because everybody wanted this place for rational considerations: it was more centrally located than the other one we found, it was bigger, it was more convenient, close to the underground and the buses. So I said, "Yeah, maybe everybody's right," and I put...

SP: Okay, you made a mistake.

Francesca (female): Yeah.

SP: But you can still fix it. You simply say, "In this location I cannot contribute—I stop, because I don't like the place." He will still use his 50% time allowance to work there, and you just pull out.

Francesca (female): This is possible. But I will miss some of the pleasure because there are things that happen in the center which I enjoy, like meeting the people.

SP: But don't work there, that's all I'm saying. You can be a participant, a visitor.

Francesca (female): Actually what I would like to do is just go to the meditations. Since the center opened, I have not been meditating anymore. Because there are always other things to do. I'm thinking, "Oh, it's Kundalini time, while everybody's doing Kundalini meditation I can fix a few things."

SP: You will have to look into how much time the male can give to the center alone, and how much is your own time for participating.

Francesca (female): The one occasion when I really had fun was when we organized... actually they organized, I just sent the e-mails... an event of magic. Many people came and the atmosphere was very nice... people lining up to have tarot readings and hand readings. And I was just behaving, you know, like a lady at a party.

SP: This is your new job, to be a lady at parties.

Francesca (female): Actually, I didn't want to go away—I stayed until the very end. Nothing was required of me, just they asked me if I could be present. I didn't have to do anything in particular and I really enjoyed that.

SP: Did you hear me when I just said, this is your new job?

Francesca (female): Yes. Lady at parties.

SP: How do you feel about your new job?

Francesca (female): I like that.

SP: You like it?

Francesca (female): Of course I do (laughing), but part of me feels guilty.

SP: Guilty about relaxing?

Francesca (female): My mind has so many arguments.

SP: Keep expressing them.

Francesca (female, sniffling from tears): How do I support myself?

SP: You're still teaching.

Francesca (female): It's too little.

SP: He (referring to the male) is organizing trainings.

Francesca (female): For the everyday life, it's not enough.

SP: Are you still paying for the boyfriend with whom you share a flat? Is he paying his half of the expenses yet?

Francesca (female): No, not yet.

SP: Would the money you earn from organizing and from teaching be enough if Stefano paid half?

Francesca (female): Yes, it would be enough.

SP: I can tell you from my personal experience that when you relax, life will surprise you.

Francesca's female is starting to cry.

SP: With your eyes closed, just breathe into this feeling that existence will provide… Keep breathing… And while you keep breathing and keep feeling, I just want to say that it's a survival problem we are looking at today. You don't really believe that you can relax this much. So this breathing is to allow you to relax more than you thought possible… Keep breathing…

You believe that without some "doing" there won't be enough money... Just keep breathing, and open to a new possibility, that survival will be possible if you are a Lady at a Party. Survival will be possible if you choose Kundalini meditation. Survival will be possible if you don't work at the center at all, only the male side works there. That means you can go to the center when you want to, and not go when you don't want to.

Francesca (female): I see one difficulty. Monday is my working day—in reality it's his. But when I go on other days, people will ask me to help with this and that.

SP: You can say to them that you are available for practical questions only on Mondays.

Francesca (female): I need to make this commitment to myself very strongly. I really need to be centered when somebody calls me into the practical side of things.

SP: It's important that you tell your male side what you are going to do with your 50% of the time. For example, you can tell him, "I am going to go to the meditations when I feel like it. I am going to be available only on Mondays..."

Francesca's female does this in Italian. She speaks about chatting with people, about going more into nature. She suggests that they enjoy nature together sometimes.

Change over.

SP (to the male): I want you to look into her eyes again, are they still open? Do you see anything different in the eyes?

Francesca (male): Yes, very different. She's human again!

Next, the session moves on into the questions of work. The female, who earns the basic money by teaching, has cut back too much on her own fun. She really wants to give two or three massages a week, not so much for money as for her own pleasure.

The male's work, on the other hand, needs some trimming because he is doing too much center work for free. He should not take charge of the group program as a whole, but organize only two or three groups per year. Then his work would be general administration in the center on Mondays, organizing three groups per year, organizing two trainings outside the center. This is not very much, he says. He would like to translate, but actually his interest is more wide than that—what he really likes to do is connect to people in foreign languages. He likes to talk in English! It's my feeling that any increase in financial power is going to come from the male.

> *SP* (to the female): Now that you have a broader picture, I want to ask you again, why did you close? Why did you stop doing the things that you enjoy?
> *Francesca* (female): Because he started to take on the responsibility for the whole center! This was not really his job, but he took it on anyway. And I was against it.
> *SP:* Did you tell him?
> *Francesca* (female): No, but anyway he wouldn't have listened.

Change over to the male.

> *SP:* Do you agree with her, that you wouldn't listen?
> *Francesca* (male): Not really. Next time she should really yell! I will listen.

I say to the female that we should see this whole thing as a growing, not as a setback. She was actually relaxing, slowly slowly, about the survival issue. And she relaxed so much that she allowed the male this grand experiment, involving much time and effort for which he earned no money. And he has learned something about himself from it. He has learned to set limits. And he has learned that the female's happiness matters to him. Now he is more ready to take financial responsibility than he was before. These things could only happen because the female had enough trust. She trusted him; she can still trust him, and now she can simply extend this trust to herself as well.

Here's another sample of an inner relationship that improves. This client was visiting me for the first time. She had very little previous experience of working on herself, but she was connected to a spiritual teacher, a different one than Osho.

Squeezed in a narrow niche

Elena comes from a small village near the Italian town of Asti. She must be about 40 years old, but she looks older because there is strain in the face and the eyes are puffy, sad, and serious. She is a midwife (*ostetrica* in Italian), and while we are just chatting before the session, she says that she really enjoys this job.

Once we start the session, I learn a bit more about her past. She has three children, each from a different man, and the youngest child is around 7 years old. The father of the youngest left her one year ago, so they were in relationship for more than six years. And when he was gone, she "chose to feel the pain" (she is crying while she says this). But she has not come to the session about that man in particular, she says, but about the pattern that repeats with men.

When she finished high school at age 20—because she was not so good at studying—she enrolled in a university to pursue the subject of geology but dropped out shortly. Most of her energy at that time went toward boyfriends, and when she met the man she would marry she moved out of her parents' house and into his house and became pregnant. They stayed together about five years, and then he left her. The next man, father to the second child, left immediately after the birth of the child.

Around age 30, she decided to pursue the profession of midwife because "mothering" was what she was best at doing. By the time she was 35 she had completed the degree and all the training involved.

I ask Elena if she has experience in meditation, or if she knows what meditation is. She says "I think so. I do a sitting meditation that has movements of the head and a word I'm supposed to say, and it lasts precisely 17 minutes." I laugh because that certainly is precise!

So we begin an energy check, where she is lying on her back on my massage table. I touch the left foot to contact the female figure. I can see her easily, a mother with children. But the children arrive to the mother in a strange way, as if she needs them, as if she is a magnet drawing them toward her and then they are stuck by her side. I see this mother in a receptive or "silent" space and the children quite active, lively, playful. To me, these are both signs that the mother is dependent on the children, and that they are taking the place of the man in her life (a common problem in Italy).

When I go next to the right foot, the male figure is also easy to see. He is "squeezed out," as if the mother and her brood are taking all the space and he has a very narrow niche to exist in. He has to contract his arms and legs just to fit between the two walls! I feel him buzzing in outrage but he is not expressing any rebellion, just looking miserable. An energetic person, I must say, but with lined face and cramped muscles.

When Elena is back in her chair, we start the experiential part of the session by covering her right eye with a blindfold. She is looking at me out of the left eye, the "female" eye, and the female answers my questions about responsibility for certain decisions in life. It is she who chose to come to the session today. It is she who chose to attend a rebirthing group recently. When she was 20 she didn't want to go to university, she just wanted to play around. She didn't feel like taking responsibility for herself until her first child was born. It was she who chose the profession of midwife and she likes it very much. About the 17-minutes meditation she is only involved occasionally, not always. In general, she chooses how she wants her life to be.

When I ask for three words which represent her, she lists 'mother', 'tired', and 'big'. Her main priorities in life are 1) love; 2) children, especially her own three children; and 3) nature. I ask her if she is succeeding in fulfilling the last priority, and she nods yes: she has a house next to a forest.

Changing the blindfold so that her male eye can see out and

the female eye is covered, Elena now answers similar questions from her male side. It was he who chose geology as a study, because he wanted to be close to the earth. He loves the earth. Actually, he was really interested in gardening. When he found out that geology was still too far away from the earth to suit him, he dropped out of the university. He likes to work with his hands, he tells me. He likes materials such as stone or wood—especially wood. He shrinks back at the mention of a job in construction, but relaxes again when he considers being a handyman. He likes very much to fix things around the house.

When I ask him if he wanted children he says "no." When I ask him if he ever told the female about this, he took a long time before answering: "No, I didn't tell her." And why not? With tears in his eyes he says that he wanted to give her what she wanted, even if it meant he could not have what he wanted. So in this way I find out that he sacrificed himself, thinking it was love, and I explain that it was not love. It has only increased the female's ego-identification, and in that sense having children was not good for her, so he should have been more insistent for his standpoint.

He is not involved in the job of midwife. That is not the type of work he likes. When asked for three words that represent him, he says 'able', 'no space', 'disturbed'. His priorities in life? Priority 1) is work... I check again if he means handyman or midwife, and he says "only handiwork." Priority 2) is more space, and priority 3) is tranquility—which he doesn't feel right now. But he jumps immediately back to priority number two, saying with vehemence, "I really need more space!" I certainly agree with him, because he cannot have his first priority without the second.

Now the interviews have ended, and I set up the pair. While Elena is sitting on the female chair with her eyes closed, I describe this female person according to what I have seen in the left leg and according to what she told me. It goes like this:

"This person's first word in describing herself was the word 'mother'. But in her case the relationship to the children is a dependent one. She doesn't realize it, because she thinks she is loving and caring for their welfare. But actually, she would never allow anyone to take the children away from her." (She tosses her head indicating a stubborn, willful concordance, that nobody can ever take the kids away from her.) I describe these children as being like baby ducks following behind a mother duck, and Elena chuckles at the image and says aloud *una coda*, which means 'tail' in Italian. "This woman has love," I say, "and her first priority is love, but she doesn't realize yet that love is a state of being which she can have all the time, whether anybody else is there or not." I also mention that when you love a man, he can go away when he wants. But with children, they have to stay with you by necessity so you have a certain power over them. The female nods that she understands the danger I am indicating.

Elena leaves the female chair and seats herself on the opposite side, in the male chair. Now she is a man, and "he" is to describe the female from a man's point of view. The male says that the female is beautiful, he sees her body quite rounded. She is expansive, much larger than him, and he sees her with the children. When I ask him to describe how he feels when he is with such a person, he says, "She is unreachable. (Pause) When she is unreachable, I feel sad, I feel like I don't exist. I could go away but then she will really forget that I exist, so I stay here. (Sigh) Actually, I don't even want to go on existing."

Change over. Elena sits in the female chair again, and the female is asked to describe how she sees the male in the other chair. She says, "It's really difficult to see him." I say, "He needs more space. Would you be willing to reduce your present job of midwife to just half the time, and give him the other half of the working hours for his own activities?" She purses her lips for a moment, and then says yes, she can agree for that.

Change over. The male side feels immediately brighter, bigger—so he reports to me. I tell him that he must start expressing his need and claiming his right to take half of the space. This time I did it for him, but in future, if she forgets, he has to clearly insist or simply take the body toward his objectives. Shrinking and going into a suicidal mode does not help anyone, whereas this bigger, happier energy he has now helps everyone. And what does he want to do with the space? First he will do a couple of jobs on his property. There are certain walls on top of a hillside that need to be repaired, for a start. He would like to work with a male partner, either as an exchange or by giving a small payment.

Change over. I say to the female side, "In case you don't realize it, half of the money that you have earned as midwife belongs to him. Are you willing to let him spend it the way he wants?" She is definitely surprised, and reports that she shrinks in size when I say this. But after considering the question a bit longer, she says yes. She has tears in her eyes as she admits that she never saw that he wanted to do something different, and she is really deeply sorry that he didn't have the chance before.

Change over. I ask the male figure to keep going with how he wants to create the life. He wants to go into town twice a week, and I pressure him to give me the exact day and hours for his first excursion. It will be next Wednesday afternoon, from 3–6 pm.

Change over. She says, "Well, the children will need looking after." But then she agrees to find a babysitter.

Change over. I ask the male if she is still unreachable. He answers no. We discuss for a moment the fact that before, she was unreachable because she was "mother," locked into a fixed role and therefore not really herself, not really available to this moment. I say, why don't you ask her to go dancing with you some evening, just the two of you, without any children... would you like that? He says yes, he would like to do that.

Change over. The female agrees, so I move the male's chair one meter backward, away from the family, and move the female chair in front of his as a symbol of being together in some kind of party place, a bar or nightclub. The female, from her chair, reports that in this moment there are no children and she is no longer a mother, but she feels good.

Something in that communication, a feeling that she now depends on him to feel good, convinces me to try another experiment. We pretend that the male sees another woman at this party place with whom he wants to spend a few moments, and I move his chair next to the new woman, symbolizing that choice. I ask the female to tell me how she feels when he does that. It takes her a while to be honest, but then she says, "I'm angry." My response: "Aha! You drop the identification of mother, but take on another identification: partner."

Bringing forth a photo of my master Osho, I ask the female to look at it and to tell me if the anger increases or decreases. It decreases, and she starts to understand what is the state of love I have been talking about… that she has it even when her so-called partner—the "other," the male—is busy doing something else.

Change over. The male has been talking to another woman, and I ask him to notice that the female (who is sitting at some distance) is quite okay. Is it new? Yes, he answers, this is new. I ask him now to choose exactly the place in the room where he would like to be, without considering her wishes but just deciding according to what is inside himself. He moves over to the window in the session room and looks outside, with his back to the female.

Change over. I ask the female how she feels. She has stopped breathing, and finally she reports that she is afraid that if he is so free, he will leave her. I answer that this is a memory from the past. And before, when he left her temporarily, having something else to do, she got angry, pretended he didn't exist, and put the children in his place. But this is all over now. It is a new moment.

I ask her to close her eyes and go to the state where she feels love. This she is able to do rather easily now, as she is actually quite a loving person. I say to the female, "Normally when the male is following his nature, you will feel him with you. But this man has not had enough chance to be himself yet. He needs more practice. You will have to trust that by and by you will feel his presence in your heart, but not yet." She says, "I don't know if I can be so alone." Again I bring the photo of Osho in front of her view, and then she sits more upright and says with some spirit, "Yes, I can do it!"

Elena commented afterwards that what she had seen inside herself exactly reflected each of the three relationships in her life.

Of course!

Awareness changes everything

Do you remember the session of Leonard, which we only started but didn't finish? In chapter six we became acquainted with his two parts by setting up the pair. Perhaps we are ready now for the next installment.

To give you a brief summary of the story so far, the masculine side of Leonard is not able to rest unless he has solved any technical problem placed in front of him, so he is doing 100% of the work—which is to design the engines for cars. He would like to be more involved in other activities but he has not yet made the change. The feminine is shy and dependent on him. She is in the habit of receiving orders and following them, a kind of servile attitude, and so she has low self-esteem and doesn't take proper care of herself physically. If you feel like entering more fully into the details again, you can reread the end of chapter six.

We'll start where we left off.

A special gift for design, second episode

Leonard has just moved to the position of the witness, and he is observing the two characters which have just described each other.

> *Leonard* (witness): It makes me a bit sad. They don't fit together.
> *SP:* Do you think they are married?
> *Leonard:* They don't need to be married, but they act like it—an old, long connection.

SP: The male side could take his freedom easily, but the female wants to continue in an automatic way with the old work. And he is saying, "I won't leave you. I will sacrifice my life to stay with you." That's why I would say they appear to be married. And personally I feel she is much more aware of what she's doing than she admits. If the session shows that she's actually conscious of what she's doing, he should not allow it anymore. He should separate, take his things and live his own choices. He should just say, "You've been dominating me long enough, and I don't go for it anymore." But let's see... You can sit there.

I am indicating the masculine chair, and so Leonard changes from the witnessing chair to become the male once again.

SP: I'm going to ask you two questions. First, are you married?
Leonard (male): It looks like, yes.
SP: Would you be ready to get a divorce and be more independent?
Leonard (male): Ja, I don't have anything to lose, actually.

Leonard goes over to the chair of the feminine.

SP (to the female): Are you married to him?
Leonard (female, very soft spoken): Yes, in a way.
SP: And how would it be for you, if he got a divorce?
Leonard (female): (she's very slow to answer) Now comes the old trick. I say "I don't care." But I see that... if I had heard the same question some years ago, I wouldn't have seen it. But now I can see that it's a trick, there's something else behind. Behind is fear, the fear to be alone.

After waiting some time for her to continue, I speak again.

SP: And now, what's happening now? How do you feel now about his choosing to get a divorce?
Leonard (female, very introspectively): I try to figure out how it is to be alone. I'm thinking about it... (glancing at me) Now I'm breathing again. I start to relax, I'm not so tense as before. But this aloneness is making me a bit insecure.

SP: To be insecure is very positive. I know you've not been thinking that before. But it means that nothing you've known already will be repeated, that life will not be boring. If you don't know how it's going to be tomorrow, there's a reason to be awake. There's a reason to be looking forward.

Leonard (female): I get the feeling I'm too simple, so I don't understand.

SP: Is that a trick, also?

She smiles like someone whose ruse has just been uncovered...
   Change over.

SP (to the male): I would like you to move your chair to a place that represents getting divorced from her and making your own space, your own home. It doesn't mean that there's no love for her, it just means that you have your own territory. You won't be living in the same house anymore, and you'll meet when you want to. Do you like that? (Leonard is reluctant to start.) Whenever you want to meet her, you can. Whenever you don't want to meet her, you'll have your own space. (He still doesn't move.) Is there something in you that prevents this?

Leonard (male): No, I want! (He tries a new location but looks unsatisfied)

SP: It has to be a place where you feel surrounded by yourself, where there's no link to somebody else.

Leonard (male): I'll have to try different places.

He tries a place with his back to the female, then says it's not right. Finally he chooses a place somewhat behind the witness chair, and facing the therapist chair.
   Change over.

SP (to the female): So, he has moved into his own house. How is it for you?

Leonard (female): Empty. (There is complaint in her voice, the old listlessness and sadness we've seen already.)

SP: Oh, really? Sounds quite terrible.

Leonard (female): (She smiles mischievously at my joke, realizing that I don't believe her.) Actually, it's okay. This moment alone is okay.

SP: Why did you say it's empty when the truth is that it's okay?

Leonard (female): It's a trick.

SP: Tell me about the trick. I want to hear all your tricks.

Leonard (female): It's a habit of negativity. The negativity is to keep other people connected to me. If I'm down, if I'm feeling bad, they will feel guilty.

SP: Uh-huh, and then they won't go away because you are feeling bad.

Leonard (female): Yeah... It's hard to accept it, to see it.

The story continues in the next and final chapter. But now that the secret of the female is out in the open, the relation between the two parts of Leonard will surely change for the better. Awareness changes everything.

CHAPTER 12

Insecurity as an Adventure

In the last chapter, I was speaking to Leonard's female about insecurity and she pretended not to understand. There is a gap in our communication, but not because she is "too simple." The reason is because she is a "fear" type rather than a "trust" type—you'll remember that I mentioned these two attitudes in chapter three.

Energy can go in two directions—contraction or expansion. It never stays neutral. Either you shrink, and pull your periphery smaller and smaller in defense because you assume the environment is dangerous, or you expand, letting your periphery get wider and wider as you perceive the environment to be friendly.

Deep in the unconscious we take a decision whether to be protected or to be vulnerable. And, as I said before, the majority of people choose the stance of protection. To them, life looks dangerous. You can die any moment—in an automobile crash, in an earthquake, or in the Twin Towers. And before you die there are even worse things that could happen: you could be sick and ruined by the hospital bills. You could be accused unjustly and put in a jail. Or, more to the point, your girlfriend could leave you for your best friend. These things happen! And they are proof that life is dangerous!

I can understand Leonard's female, what kind of mind she has. But in the final installment of Leonard's session, which is presented shortly, I will call upon her to see the male's predicament. He is fettered by her determination to stay secure. He wants to experiment with trust. He wants to see what there is for him beyond computer work, beyond technical competence. He wants to love! She can hinder him or she can help him in his search for what his freedom might be like.

As she has shown a willingness to be alone, I will invite her now to have an attitude of experimentation. I will invite her to have some fun. Once she sees the advantages of risking, once she sees the beauty and strength that arise in her when she tries to launch her own projects, I don't think she can go back to sitting in the kitchen, "safe" but disheveled because she doesn't love herself.

Take courage and jump

We pick up Leonard's session after the female has admitted her strategies for keeping the male trapped.

A special gift for design, third episode

Leonard leaves the chair of the feminine and sits in the masculine chair, which now has a new position in the room.

> *SP* (to the male): Your decisions are your own now; you don't have to ask for anyone's agreement or concern yourself with the opinion of others.
> *Leonard* (male): I want to enjoy.
> *SP:* What are the things you enjoy?
> *Leonard:* I want to be outside when it's nice weather. I like to

connect with people, to spend time with them. I can be on my own, too. But I want to stop this duty that I *have* to work as an engineer, that I have always to solve technical problems.

SP: So you would quit completely the job in Düsseldorf, if you didn't have to be concerned about others.

Leonard (male): Yeah, I would stop.

SP: Do you think you can arrange things there so that you can simply stop?

Leonard (male): Not so quickly, but maybe it would be possible.

Leonard changes to the other chair.

SP (to the female): He's going to stop his job as a technician. You can also decide how you want to spend your time.

Leonard (female): (after a long pause…) I'll have to find work.

SP: Yes, I think so—you have to find work! What would you enjoy?

Leonard (female): I can do almost anything when the things aren't too complicated. I can cook, I can manage a house… but gardening is the thing that would make me most happy.

SP: Which part of gardening do you like best?

Leonard (female): To make it beautiful. To set the plants in a beautiful way.

SP: Landscaping, then.

Leonard (female): Yes.

SP: Great idea. You are an artist, it sounds like.

Leonard (female): Yeah (a little unconvinced).

SP: You're interested in beauty?

Leonard (female): Let's say I care how it looks. (pause) Yeah… I don't care so much about myself, about how I look, but how it looks around me is important. If it's a room I care about the furniture, pictures, paintings…

SP: Interior decorator!

Leonard (female): Yes.

SP: Uh-huh. So you *are* an artist.

Leonard (female): It's the same as with the garden. I care if the color combination is nice.

SP: Would you like to have your own company for doing these things, or would you prefer to work for somebody else who has the structure already set up? For example, there are landscaping companies that you could join.

Leonard (female): I would like to try to do it on my own. I'm not sure that I can manage. But it's more interesting to have perhaps a bit more responsibility. When somebody is saying to me where to put the plants and then I do it, I lose my creativity. My own part in it is gone.

SP: I understand you very well. I'm happy that you want to decide where the plants go, that you don't want to take somebody's order.

Change over.

SP (to the male): Okay. Do you think you did her a favor by getting a divorce?

Leonard (male): Yes.

SP: What do you see as the positive outcome?

Leonard (male): We could work as partners. In my old business she couldn't contribute anything because she is not a technical person. In this new field, she can contribute at least half—and me too, I can contribute what I'm good at, what I like. And I do it for myself. But the biggest change I see in her is that she's taking her part of the responsibility. And now I won't let myself be hooked in when she becomes sad.

SP: I would like you to speak to her now, to tell her that you're not going to stop yourself anymore just because she's sad.

Leonard (male): I'm a little afraid—I don't know how she'll respond.

Change over.

SP (to the female): My feeling is that he'd like to visit you, but he's a little bit nervous because of the past. Can you understand?

Leonard (female): (whispered) Yes.

SP: Right now you're a strong person, with your own abilities. And the minute he comes around there's a chance that you will go back to complaining that you don't know what to do, that you will follow orders, and you will become sad when he leaves you for a while. How could you establish your new identity a little more clearly for yourself, so that you don't lose it?

Leonard (female): I need time. I need to start some activities so I have more trust that I can manage this step.

We spend some moments considering how she could establish her new profession, how she could announce it to other people.

Leonard (female): You know, these are things that I have done in the past but I have never been paid for it.

SP: I don't see any reason why you shouldn't be paid, you have a natural talent! So many people need your assistance; many people have a taste for beauty but they don't know how to manifest it. Don't you think, perhaps, that your small trust has to do with a historical fact? That women have always been doing many things for which they don't get paid, for example working in the house?

Leonard (female): Yes, partly.

SP: Making a step backwards, because I just remembered something... Before, I got the feeling that you were forcing the inner man to continue his work as an engineer. Were you?

Leonard (female): I guess so... because he had to feed both of us, so actually I was forcing him.

SP: I noticed that somebody went two weeks too late to cancel the office contract, so then it had to be extended a whole year more. Did you do that on purpose?

Leonard (female): No, I didn't do it consciously; I was unaware. But I had hopes that the business would flow again. Yes, I wanted to keep the office. Because if he had the possibility to cancel the office then he might make bigger changes... I also felt this.

SP: Now, imagine that you can call him on the telephone—I mean, he's living over there in his house. What would you say to him, regarding what you just discovered?

Leonard (female): It's hard to talk to him about the office.

Even if I was not very conscious, and not aware that I did it on purpose, still I'm ashamed.

SP: Maybe he will forgive you… easily.

Leonard (female): Maybe he gets angry.

SP: Let's see! I will help you. If he gets angry, I'll protect you. I have every interest in preserving this artist because she has something very precious in her capacity to make things beautiful, and I don't want her smashed. It's very simple: you just apologize for wanting to depend on him for such a long time. But do it in your own words.

Leonard (female, to the male): I'm a bit ashamed to say this. I'm sorry that I have done tricks to keep you close to me because I was afraid to be alone. I tried to keep our life as it was before, and not to allow any change. I was not aware. I'm sorry. Now I'm going to try to develop my own things, and I think I will be more happy.

Change over.

Leonard (male): I don't want to blame you. I'm pleased with the situation—to have this distance. I feel more relaxed. What was yesterday, and the day before yesterday, can't be changed. The important thing is what we have now. It relaxes me that you start to find your own creativity.

The "way" is inside

I've gone to such lengths to present the entire session of Leonard, in three parts, because this session shows very clearly the procedure for helping the polarities, male and female, to stand on their own legs. We started to look at this procedure already in chapter six. After I set up Leonard's pair, I asked you quite a few questions.

For example, I asked you if this session belonged to the resonance pattern type 1, type 2, or type 3.

Now I will tell you my own analysis. When I started to give this session, I thought the session was type number 1—both polarities non-resonant in the feet, but supported by resonance elsewhere in the body. However, sensing the truth in what the male side wanted to do with his life, I decided for number 2, in which one of the partners (the male) is already "connected" inside but believes that he has to adapt to the other. And then things changed some more, when the female part showed the capacity to be alone and made serious attempts to drop her dependency. The session became type 3. So whatever answer you picked, 1, 2, or 3, it was right!

I say all this because I'm going to describe next how the therapist chooses the intervention. If you think this isn't interesting for you, you can skip down to the next section. But probably it will not be difficult to understand my theoretical (and practical) explanation, as you already have Leonard's session as a reference.

How we would intervene with Leonard has a certain logic: it depends on which number we choose as the maximum potential of the session. With type number 1, the aim of the session would be to bring the strongest character (Leonard's male part) into aloneness, but not necessarily to find the gestures or movements that arise from that aloneness. With type 2, we would help this character to become active. So with both types 1 and 2, we would work only with a single character, the stronger one. We would leave the weaker figure (Leonard's female part) untouched. But at that moment when Leonard's female shows an ability to tolerate the distance from the male and to accept her aloneness, our session makes a jump to a superior category, number 3. With this type of session the aim is to help the second figure (the female) expand into its newly discovered independence.

If, in working with an inner couple, you have decided to set up the pair because there is enough resonance, then your first challenge is to choose which figure you will focus on during the session. It is an important moment, because you will be inviting that character to go "in," and you have to be fairly sure that he or she can manage!

Once you have chosen the character, you have to take this character only two steps: first to aloneness, then to creativity.

In the first step, the aloneness you are looking for is not the aloneness of withdrawal, isolation, or separateness. It is an aloneness where the character is glad to be himself (or herself), glad for whatever is happening inside. It's the therapist's job to determine, during the resonance check, if such a joyful presence—the same thing as meditative ability—is already there. If yes, then this inner integrity, this beauty, can be revealed to the person. You can see that I have done that for certain characters presented in this book, Bettina's male, Charlotte's female, Michael's female, Marco's male, just to name a few.

Once the character is feeling okay alone, you invite him (or her) to see that actually nothing inhibits him from using his space in whatever way he would enjoy. Before, when he was hooked to the opposite figure through desire, he was making all kinds of compromises and often letting the other one, which was itself in darkness, choose the path to follow. Now that the interior partner has become a secondary influence, this character makes the choices for himself (or herself). He has to be responsible on all levels, particularly for the ground level of survival, but also for the sustenance of the heart.

So these are the two steps: first to *be* and then to let this being have its natural flow. As I never get tired of repeating, this ability to *be* is a nourishment for the opposite character, who then relaxes in the new atmosphere. In the end we have two individuals. They don't meet because they are inextricably tied to each other. They meet because their essential being is already a single, unified presence. And it has always been so.

They don't have to *try* to meet. They only need the courage to step into the unknown each moment on their own tracks, to be each one insecure. Leonard's session is a clear example of this. The male's track is to leave computer work and enter into more emotionally rewarding contacts with people and with nature. The female's track is to be paid for her ability as a decorator. And of course there is no guarantee that they will be safe in their journeys. Quite the opposite. But one thing is sure: they will grow.

By growth, I mean that in each one the inner kernel of love, of self-satisfaction, of happiness is expanding, becoming ever wider. And by growth, I mean that each one's trust in his or her natural impulses is so deep that the opposite polarity's wishes are no longer absorbed as restrictions. But for this they first need to let go of each other, they need to be free. And although it sounds simple, there can be some resistance.

Cultivating the sense of freedom

We all say that we want to be free. It's true, but only as an ideal. In actual fact, we would like to avoid responsibility for the consequences that freedom implies. We would like freedom, but together with security. We would like to feel free, but with everything around ourselves staying as it is. For example, we would like to express our creativity but without the irksome bother of changing job, or house, or friends. Do you see the catch? If somebody indicates to us the path toward freedom we refuse it—but in a very polite way, of course.

By coincidence, I recently worked with a very interesting client who this year received an award as "Woman of the Year" among

Italian entrepreneurs. She, along with two other women, has created an association having the social aim to serve women and children, and by now it has become famous. She is the president—well, truthfully, her male side is the president, and his work is organization and finance. Her female side is not working. The female side is a child, only three years old. She is basically playing around, being too young for job, and what she likes best in life is "being free." The male side is doing 100% of the work, not only supporting the female side but also the two business partners who are similar to the female. So, if you count himself, he is supporting four people! Plus taking care of three children, because the female side is not involved in that work either. Naturally, being so overworked has had its consequences: my client (in reality, her male side) ended up in the hospital for removal of the gall bladder.

Now, the inner female wanted the inner male to stay exactly the same; she told me—proudly—that she had no criticisms of him whatsoever. And she thought the past ten years in the business had been just great up to now. What was the need for any change?

It was a challenge for me to help this female understand that she was asking for freedom without responsibility, and that her attitude was leading to an impending disaster. She should drop this habit of depending on someone else. Slowly slowly she started to wake up a little bit. She had to, because the male was on the verge of doing things differently—or, let's say, he found himself unable to continue as before.

My work consists in inviting each of the two characters that we have inside, the male and the female, to realize what is their natural pathway—that is, in which direction they are naturally inclined when they take responsibility for being happy. I try to create an atmosphere that permits them to do this without fear. When they are each on their own path, they will surely find self-love, and then they will love each other also just because love has become their climate.

I hope that this book and the stories it contains have given you a glimpse of how love and freedom accompany each other. Such an enduring love is possible, but it requires a sincere commitment on your part, the certainty that you want to grow, and the willingness to experiment with techniques and life situations that could be of assistance.

Once the commitment is there, I can guarantee you an exciting ride. The breeze won't let your boat stand still for long.

About the Author

Sagarpriya DeLong was born in Tacoma, Washington, U.S.A. She studied music and philosophy at Carleton College, and graduated with honors in 1968. The ferment of those times led her to New York's Lower East Side, where she worked with teenagers from the housing projects, and then to the Esalen Institute in Big Sur, California, where she joined the massage team and eventually became director of the massage program.

Esalen was, in the late 1960s, the first and maybe the only personal growth center in America, and many brilliant innovators in the field of humanistic psychology had gathered there: Ida Rolf, Fritz Perls, Will Schutz, Charlotte Selvers, Alan Watts, just to name a few. Sagarpriya—at that time known as Roberta DeLong Miller—absorbed from these people an understanding of the connection between body and spirit, and in 1975 she published her first book, *Psychic Massage*, about the subtle psychological information one can feel while touching the body. This book became a classic which remained in print for the next twenty years.

By the age of thirty, Sagarpriya had a successful career as a group leader in massage, meditation, and centering. She was traveling throughout America, also to England and Holland. She started to notice that her acquaintances in Europe were gradually "disappearing" into India, never to be heard of again, and she learned that they were meditating with an Indian mystic, Osho.

When she finally met Osho in 1977, she understood why: this man radiated an extraordinary quality of love that would be very hard to describe in words.

Sagarpriya became a *sannyasin*, a seeker of truth. She stayed as close to Osho as she could—first in India, then in the United States, then again in India until his death in 1990. During this period she invented many new group therapies: "Urja" (energy), "Wu-Wei" (action through inaction), "The Real Man Standing There" (working from no-effort). She helped to develop both basic and advanced Therapist Trainings, which she coordinated for many years. Finding that her work attracted a large following in Japan, she created a Therapist Training for Japanese specifically suited to their culture. Sagarpriya's counseling trainings have graduated more than 300 therapists presently active in twenty-five countries.

Around the year 1987, Sagarpriya began the development of a new kind of therapeutic work called Star Sapphire. As she could see her involvement in Psychic Massage coming to a natural conclusion, she wrote a final and definitive book on the subject, *The Master's Touch*, in order to preserve that body of knowledge intact. The English version was published in 1995, with subsequent translations in Japanese, Chinese, Italian, Russian, and German languages.

Her therapy trainings changed slowly, slowly, departing from the subject of counseling in general and moving to the specific Star Sapphire technique. Star Sapphire typically uses a dialogue between the male and female aspects to come in tune with oneself. *The two shores of Love* is her first book about this method.

Sagarpriya now lives in Italy. She is a co-founder of Conscious Living, an association based in Imola, near Bologna. Conscious Living offers trainings in Star Sapphire Energywork and Psychic Massage, and also seminars related to consciousness in daily life. Sagarpriya's email is sagarpriya@consciousliving.it.

CPSIA information can be obtained
at www.ICGtesting.com
Printed in the USA
BVOW00s0337111116
467492BV00010BA/40/P